JACK LONDON

Essays in Criticism

JACK LONDON
Essays in Criticism

Edited by
Ray Wilson Ownbey

Peregrine Smith, Inc.
SANTA BARBARA AND SALT LAKE CITY

1978

Library of Congress Cataloging in Publication Data

Main entry under title:

Jack London, essays in criticism.

Bibliography: p.
1. London, Jack, 1876-1916—Criticism and interpretation—Addresses, essays, lectures. I. Ownbey, Ray Wilson, 1936- II. Title.
PS3523.046Z652 818'.5'209 78-26193
ISBN 0-87905-053-5

Manufactured in the United States of America

Contents

Jack London

Introduction: London in the Seventies

RAY OWNBEY

Jack London's eldest daughter Joan said that her father was a member of the last frontier generation. His life touched two centuries, and was fraught with contradiction. He was a believer in the survival of the fittest, but very generous to a large family of dependents. He was the socialist from the lower classes who fought against class distinctions, but who employed an Oriental houseboy. He was the robust, muscular man of hard work and experience who was perfectly willing to cater to the whims and pruderies of Victorian morality and whose best friend was an aristocratic poet, George Sterling. And he was the highly principled writer who spent much of his career grinding out fiction whose merit lay primarily in its ability to produce income rather than artistic or critical acclaim. In spite of, or perhaps because of these incongruities, London's life and his works take us roaring into the twentieth century.

London's writing career, which started with the publication of "To the Man on the Trail" in 1899 and ended with his death in 1916, maintained the energetic voice which we associate with the growing American nation of the nineteenth century, but it also contained the voice of the reformer, the disillusioned idealist who would change that world into a better one. This voice, very much a part of the American tradition of reformers who followed, turned from the romance of the Klondike to the disgust of the city and the conflict between the individual and society. In his later works, London wrote of a return to the land, to the simple virtues of the rural life, as a solution to the ravages capitalism had brought.

London is important to us in other ways, however, than just as a transitional figure in our literature. His life has almost reached the level of legend. Probably no other American writer, except perhaps F. Scott Fitzgerald a generation later, laid bare so openly his own experience in fiction and lived so closely the life revealed in that fiction.

London enjoyed immense popularity in his lifetime. His books were widely read and the serializations of them in popular magazines gave him an audience in the days before paperback books could make him available at the drugstore. He was the first author to make a million dollars with his writing. His works have been translated into more than sixty foreign languages, and he is today immensely popular in other countries, especially the Soviet Union where he is the most widely read American author.

Critical attention to his work has been obvious by its omission, however, and London had been delegated to the literary bench by the 1950s. Robert Spiller says in *The Cycle of American Literature* that "London put power into his tales but lost control of the forces he had unleashed." He "burned himself out with the fire of his own violence."[1] In *Cavalcade of the American Novel,* Edward Wagenknecht says, "It was because he had betrayed his art that his art, at last, failed to save him from the forces that were destroying him." Wagenknecht concludes, "He was a hack writer of genius."[2]

Fred Lewis Pattee, writing in 1923 in *The Development of the American Short Story,* has, I think, a more useful if somewhat limited view of London. "It is easy to criticize him, it is easy to deplore him and even to despise him, but it is impossible to avoid him." More to the point, he says, "London's enduring work lies undoubtedly among his one hundred and fifty-two short stories."[3]

Just how do we account for the resurgence of interest in London? London is being read and written about more today than at any time in the past fifty years. Courses are being taught on London. Joan Sherman lists in *Jack London: A Reference Guide* 147 entries for the years 1950-59, 313 for 1960-69, and 281 for 1970-mid-76.[4]

There is nothing surprising about an author's popularity running in cycles. Scott Fitzgerald is read more now than at any time since the peak of his popularity in the 1920s. Herman Melville, although successful in his own lifetime, had nowhere the critical respect or the readership which has grown since the publication of *Billy Budd* in 1924, thirty-three years after his death.

One curious element in London's career which sets him apart from these other authors is the fact that although he enjoyed popular success during his lifetime, he has continued to be read throughout the decades following, but with a very limited audience. The recent criticism of London, however, treats him with the serious perspective so obviously missing during the intervening years. Critical attention is being paid to London's works as a whole—to themes, patterns, to the intellectual development of the writer, and to the writer's craft.

[1](New York: New American Library, 1956), p. 158.

[2](New York: Henry Holt and Company, 1952), pp. 226, 228.

[3](New York: Biblo and Tannen, 1923), pp. 348,351. Dale L. Walker and James E. Sisson, III list in *The Fiction of Jack London; A Chronological Bibliography* 188 stories. Another story has been published in *The Saturday Evening Post,* "Devil's Dice Box," December, 1976.

[4]Joan Sherman, *Jack London: A Reference Guide* (Boston: G.K. Hall and Co.), 1977.

Much more is being written about *Martin Eden,* for instance, than about the Klondike stories.

One conclusion from these facts is that there is a whole new group of readers of London. Serious critics are taking a second, or perhaps a first, look at the works. The question remains, how do we account for the resurgence of interest in the writer? Certainly there are scholars who can justify that interest. King Hendricks notes London's ability to create narrative, his ability to create effective atmosphere, and his masterful use of irony.[5] Earle Labor identifies London's achievement in the following areas: The Social Crusader, The Folk Writer, The Literary Craftsman, and then goes on to say that London's "ultimate greatness derives from his 'primordial vision' —the mythopoeic force which animates his finest creations and to which we respond without fully understanding why."[6]

London, in one very real sense, was a writer who was simply ahead of his time. Now we are able to deal with him as he should have been dealt with originally. There are some obvious weaknesses in this kind of oversimplified hindsight. However, there is something in such an analysis, and that something comes most clear if we look at the authors around him.

One who comes to mind is Henry James, who died in the same year as London, 1916. No two writers were ever farther apart in their backgrounds, in their subject matters, or in their styles. The other major writers at the end of the nineteenth century in America, Twain and Howells, both had careers which, like James, had peaked before London's fifteen year flash came along. These three giants, although very different from each other, differed even more from London. For one thing, London was a Westerner. The simple fact of geography indicates something about his orientation and his view of the American experience. Even Twain, who wrote with such charm and humor about the West, spent most of his adult life in Connecticut. London's subject was a more recent frontier even than Twain's, the Klondike as opposed to California. James and Howells looked either to the East or to Europe. Different from all of them is London's gusto, his self-taught, rough, only partly polished persona, which is integral to his fiction.

The writers who followed London—Sinclair Lewis, Upton Sinclair, Theodore Dreiser, the reformers, the critics of the American Dream—came later; their careers flourished in the decade following the First World War. None of them had anything like London's popular following during the first fifteen years of the century.

[5]"Jack London: Master Craftsman of the Short Story" (Logan: Utah State University, 1966), p. 11.

[6]*Jack London,* TUSAS (New York: Twayne Publishers, Inc., 1974), p. 150.

The decade of the twenties spawned other major American writers whose careers and reputations have eclipsed London or his followers: Fitzgerald, Hemingway, Faulkner. We can see in those who followed London debts to the beginnings he made. Hemingway's simplicity of style and rugged masculinity, Dreiser's disillusionment with the American Dream, even the macho narrative of Norman Mailer or James Jones—all these might well pay a tribute to London.

Some attention is necessary here to London's contribution to the development of American naturalism. Certainly if we look at London in relation to other American naturalists, Stephen Crane and Frank Norris before London, and Theodore Dreiser after, London stands out as different from and perhaps more influential and representative than any of them. London's importance as a naturalist rests partly with his unique position chronologically in American literature, as discussed above, but also with the fact that he embodies, both in his life and in his writing, the contradictions in American naturalism.

On the one hand is the biological determinist who might, if consistent, advocate a complete laissez-faire capitalism, a system where the fit would, indeed, survive economically as well as biologically, where the weak would be destroyed as they are in nature. But on the other hand is London the optimistic Marxian socialist who would use political means to take power away from the greedy capitalists who control the wealth, and redistribute it among the workers.

Perhaps the best example of this contradiction is in the character of Wolf Larson in *The Sea Wolf*, for here is a character who is the very embodiment of the "blond beast," the superman whose survival is based on his strength, both physically and morally. But it is in that moral strength that Larson becomes interesting, for he is an idealist, a man whose strength extends to mental and intellectual pursuits as well as physical ones. Certainly he is a more stunning representative of the naturalistic man than is the pitiful, though strong dullard in Norris's *McTeague* or the quiet innocent in Crane's *The Red Badge of Courage*.

Wolf Larson is the virile embodiment of the contradictions Charles Child Walcutt identifies in *American Literary Naturalism: A Divided Stream*. Walcutt says that the contradictions in naturalistic writing have in them

> the tension between hope and despair, between rebellion and apathy, between defying nature and submitting to it, between celebrating man's impulses and trying to educate them, between embracing the universe and regarding its dark abysses with terror.[7]

[7](Minneapolis: University of Minnesota Press, 1956), p. 17.

There are other elements which mark the importance of London's influence on American naturalism. Perhaps the one thing which sets him apart from the other naturalists is the very simple element of his good nature. There is a kind of hope, of playfulness in London's life which, in spite of the grim facts of many of his stories, overcomes the sordid environmental and biological determinism so common in naturalistic writing. There is also a vigorous love of life in London, that in spite of his racism, his sexism, and his muscular stance permeates both his life and his writings. Perhaps the author himself is the best example of the possibilities for the naturalistic hero.

These elements burned out in London's writing. A book from his late career, such as *The Valley of the Moon,* because of its romantic optimism, has nowhere the strength as *The Sea Wolf* or *The Call of the Wild.* His importance as a naturalist rests much more with these earlier works than with the later ones.

What emerges from this view of the writers around London is the fact that both in chronology and in the subject matter and its treatment, London stands alone. There are no other voices in the early part of the twentieth century which were looking at America from London's perspective.

A second reason for the renewed interest in London has to do with the intellectual and literary climate in this country during the sixties and seventies. For one thing, the exclusiveness, the isolation of the academic community was blasted, along with the complacency of the black ghettos, by riot and dissent. Campuses were awash with students demanding a voice and a change. This in itself may not have affected the mood or direction of literary criticism, but it was indicative of a move away from the snobbishness which characterized much of the criticism of the earlier part of the century. The wave of New Criticism with all the exclusiveness it bred was on the wane.

Along with this trend was a new kind of literature growing in America, a new proletarian literature which created an audience likely to be more receptive to London. The new proletarians were the Beatniks, who eschewed traditional values and promoted a new mysticism and a new audience—one which could read and revel in a novel like Kerouac's *On the Road,* a personal narrative chronicling the odyssey of souls out of phase with a materialistic society. This work recalls *The Road,* London's own account of his tramping experience fifty years earlier.

The differences between the Beats and London are many, most notably the fact that the Beats' road didn't go anywhere except back and forth across the country. London's road had a direction; his socialism made him a reformer, not just a chronicler of a mobile ennui. But more important is the fact that in London and the Beats we find a robustness masking a mystic vision, and it is this combination which ties them together.

Although London never abandoned his principles of socialism, in his later books, especially *The Valley of the Moon,* the world of the cities is so corrupt that his characters leave it and return to the land.[8] He says in a letter to Roland Phillips in 1911, "I am planning a serial, the motif is back to the land. While, for once in my life the story will not be offensive to bourgeois business ethics, it will at the same time be something of which I shall absolutely and passionately believe every word."[9]

The renewed interest in London is due in part to the fact that he is no longer read primarily as a children's author. For a writer to survive all those years is one thing, but for him to break out of the mold into which time has put him is quite another. Hensley Woodbridge who, with John London and George H. Tweney, compiled a monumental bibliography of London in 1966, has helped to make the transition. The *Bibliography* was reprinted with a supplement in 1973. Joan Sherman's *Jack London: A Reference Guide* was published in 1977. Critics like Franklin Walker, King Hendricks, and Earle Labor have been instrumental in bringing London out of the toy box.

There is no question now about London's growing reputation or about the interest in his works by serious readers and critics. *Western American Literature* published an entire edition on London (August, 1976), and *Modern Fiction Studies* did a special issue on London, (Spring, 1976). *The Pacific Historian* did the same, (Summer, 1977), as did *Europe* (1976).

Three biographies have recently been published: Irving Stone's fictional biography *Sailor on Horseback* was reissued with twenty-eight stories in 1977; *Jack London: The Man, The Writer, The Rebel* by Robert Barltrop was published in 1976; and *Jack: A Biography of Jack London* was published by Andrew Sinclair in 1977.

The essays in this collection represent some of the best writing done about London during the last two decades. They range from general investigations of patterns or themes in the works to rather specific analyses of particular pieces. It is hoped that the reader of London will find the impetus to read further in both the works and the criticism of this underestimated American writer.

[8]London resigned disillusioned from the Socialist Labor Party in 1916, but he retained a firm belief in the principles he claimed the Party had abandoned.

[9]King Hendricks and Irving Shephard (eds.), *Letters from Jack London* (New York: The Odyssey Press, 1965), p. 347.

Jack London:
Master Craftsman of the Short Story

KING HENDRICKS

London's reputation has rested largely on his masterful short stories. Most Americans are familiar with at least one or two of London's stories. Professor Hendricks discusses four of these stories, "To Build a Fire," "The Love of Life," "The Law of Life," and "The Chinago." The qualities identified here help the reader to understand why these stories have remained popular and why London is being read and written about today.

In November of 1898 Jack London, aged 22, sold his first short story, "To the Man on Trail," to *Overland Monthly* for the sum of $5. Three months later *The Black Cat* magazine paid him $40 for "A Thousand Deaths." This was the beginning of a writing career that in 17 years was to produce 149 short stories, not including his tramping experiences which he published under the title of *The Road*, 19 novels, and a number of essays. If all were accumulated and published, they would fill 50 volumes. Besides this, he wrote a number of newspaper articles (war correspondence, sports accounts, and sociological and socialistic essays), and thousands of letters.

He received national attention in January 1900 when *The Atlantic Monthly* published his short story, "An Odyssey of the North," and he found international acclaim when Macmillan published *The Call of the Wild* in July 1903.

Between November 1898 and July 1903 he wrote feverishly: short stories, essays, jokes, short poems, two novels (*A Daughter of the Snows* and *The Call of the Wild*), one juvenile book (*The Cruise of the Dazzler*), a sociological treatise (*The People of the Abyss*), and, with Anna Strunsky, the *Kempton-Wace Letters*. He made it a practice to

Utah State University Faculty Honor Lecture. Originally published by the Faculty Association, Utah State University. Reprinted by permission.

send his materials to editors of newspapers, magazines and publishing companies, one after another until someone accepted them.

During his life he kept record books of his magazine sales in which he listed the title of the story or essay, the magazines to which he submitted and the dates, if and when it was accepted, and the fee he received for it. Some stories were accepted by the first editor to whom they were sent; some went to several, and one, "The Story of Keesh," was rejected 24 times before *Holiday Magazine* published it in 1904.

The first two record books cover the period from November 1898 to May 1903. They include about 140 entries which garnered more than 650 rejection slips. (Most of these rejection slips are now on file in the Huntington Library.) Many are simply formal notes from editors saying that the story in question is not suitable for their purposes or that they do not have the space available. Some editors make interesting comments, and some reveal the type of material that magazines were looking for at the turn of the century. For instance, one, unidentified, written in longhand on a piece of brown paper, reads: "This type of story is absolutely impossible for us. Try *Vanity Fair* or *Town Topics*. It is in their line. We want clean, happy stories of love or incident."

Another one came from the Frank Leslie Publishing House. It does not identify the story nor the time, and simply says across a form note: "Well written. Too risque for our use." Another slip, again with no date nor any identification of the story, came from the *American Agriculturist,* and reads: "Much too long for what it tells. Same story and ideas could be expressed in fewer words." The editor of *Vogue,* on a form card which they used for rejection purposes, without date and without title of the story wrote in longhand: "Too tragic. We're open to little love stories of 1,600 words."

Perhaps his most interesting rejection slip came as a result of his first letter to an editor. He wrote it September 17, 1898 to the editor of the *Bulletin* (San Francisco) and it reads:

> Dear Sir, I have returned from a year's residence in the Klondike, entering the country by way of Dyea and Chilcoot Pass. I left by way of St. Michaels, thus making all together a journey of twenty-five thousand miles on the Yukon in a small boat. I have sailed and traveled quite extensively in other parts of the world and learned to seize upon that which is interesting and to grasp the true romance of things, and to understand the people I may be thrown amongst. I have just completed an article of four thousand words describing the trip from Dawson to St. Michaels in a rowboat. Kindly let me know if there would be any demand in your columns for it. Of course, thoroughly understanding that the acceptance of the manu-

script is to depend upon its literary and intrinsic value. Yours very respectfully, Jack London.

The editor wrote in longhand the following note on the bottom of London's letter and returned it to him. "Interest in Alaska has subsided in an amazing degree. Then again, so much has been written that I do not think it would pay us to buy your story." The story in question was called "From Dawson to the Sea." After his letter from the (San Francisco) *Bulletin,* he submitted it to the editor of *Outing,* who rejected it, to the editor of *The Examiner,* apparently the *San Francisco Examiner,* who rejected it, to the editor of *Western Press,* who rejected it, and to the editor of *Buffalo Express,* who published it on June 5, 1899 and agreed to pay him $10. There is a note in his record book that he had to dun them on July 18, 1899 to get the money.

But in spite of the many rejections, the situation during these 3 years was not as dire as it would at first seem. He published 106 items in newspapers and magazines throughout the United States. Many of the newspapers and magazines are to us today unfamiliar but some still exist, such as the *San Francisco Examiner* and *The Boston Transcript.* He published in such prominent magazines as *The Atlantic Monthly, The Youth's Companion, The Review of Reviews, McClures Magazine, Outing Magazine, Woman's Home Companion, Harper's Bazaar, The Bookman, Ainslees, Colliers, St. Nicholas,* and *Cosmopolitan,* some of which are familiar to today's readers.

It is interesting that many of these early stories are among his best. Some of his best Northland stories were written during this period. Stories such as "Batard," one of the most brutal and yet one of his most human stories; "An Odyssey of the North"; "The Law of Life," one of his best and one that I shall discuss tonight; the first version of "To Build a Fire" which I shall later discuss; "Li-Wan the Fair"; "In the Forests of the North"; "The Master of Mystery"; "The Sickness of Lone Chief"; and "The League of Old Men" were all created. For most of these he received only a pittance: $5, $10, or at most $40. There was one exception however. The *Atlantic Monthly* paid him $200 for "An Odyssey of the North."

By 1903 he was beginning to command higher prices that ranged from $40 to $120 per story. Nine years later, in 1912, Jack London signed a contract with *Cosmopolitan Magazine.* He was to furnish the magazine one short story a month for 5 years and he was to receive $1,000 for each short story. The contract also provided he furnish one novel each year for serialization, for which he would receive $12,000.

His 1912 contract with *Cosmopolitan* carried a stipend of $24,000 a year for material which he had not yet written, and yet only 10 years before editors were reluctant to print his stories, and when they did print them he was given as low as $5 per story.

But the main purpose of my paper tonight is to deal with Jack London as a master craftsman of the short story; to explore the reasons why he has been the most widely read of any American author to date; why his stories have been translated into more than 40 different languages; why he is the best known American writer in Russia, in the Scandinavian countries, in Germany and in England; why he is so popular in the Near East, why he is generally regarded as one of the greats of all time in Australia and New Zealand, and why he has sold so widely in America.

The Call of the Wild alone has sold over 2 million copies and yet London is generally ignored by students of American literature, and by English teachers throughout the country. I have been told on more than one occasion by a freshman student that his high school teacher refused to allow him to review or to report on a book or a story by Jack London. I cannot account for this attitude on the part of the English teachers of America. I can only say that most of them who find nothing in Jack London do so because they have read nothing of Jack London. The people who have read such stories as "The Love of Life" and "The Law of Life" and "The Chinago" realize that they are among the great short stories of all time.

There are several things about Jack London's better stories which make them great. He said in his first letter that he had:

> learned to seize upon that which is interesting, to grasp the true romance of things and to understand the people I may be thrown amongst.

That may be the key to his success.

A short story should have a good narrative. It should read well. It should be written in lucid and graphic style. It should deal with singular incidents and only a few characters. Too many people, too many places and too many things take it out of the realm of the short story into the realm of longer fiction. Most short stories should contain a strong element of irony. As a matter of fact, most of the great short stories of the world do have a strong ironic twist. Stories like de Maupassant's "The Necklace" or "A Piece of String" or Hardy's "The Three Strangers" live almost entirely upon ironical situations. And yet in none of these stories is there stronger irony than in some of London's stories.

A short story, when it includes description, must have strong and vivid description. London had the ability to create a strong narrative, to create marvelous story atmosphere, to infuse into it graphic descriptions that pertain to the characters or the events. But most of all, he could develop an ironical situation that, upon analysis, touches each of our lives.

For the purpose of this paper I'm going to deal with four stories of the 149. There will be many who will disagree with my choice. Many would prefer such stories as "An Odyssey of the North," some undoubtedly would prefer "Batard." Some would perhaps choose "The League of Old Men." I was tempted myself to include "A Night's Lodging," because of the irony involved. Some would prefer the South Sea stories of David Grief where there is, perhaps, more adventure. Others would prefer the stories with local color such as the "South of the Slot." But the stories I have selected will illustrate the major characteristics that I wish to point out in London's writing:

First, his tremendous ability to create a narrative, to write narration, to carry the reader from page to page through the development of the story.

Second, his ability to create an atmosphere in which the character moves and lives and which, many times, affects the outcome of the story.

Third, his masterful ability to use irony. I have mentioned the irony of de Maupassant and Hardy, and yet the irony in the stories I deal with tonight is, in many ways, as great as any.

For this purpose I have selected "To Build a Fire," "The Love of Life," and "The Law of Life," three of his Northland stories, and one from the South Seas, "The Chinago." Three of these stories were written, at least in the first version, before 1902. The other, "The Chinago," was written in 1908.

I will take the liberty to quote quite liberally from London's stories because only by that means can I illustrate what might be called his ability to graphically portray both narration and description.

To many scholars and teachers, "To Build a Fire" is Jack London's short story masterpiece. It is a masterpiece because of the depth of its irony, and its understanding of human nature, the graphic style of the writing, and the contrast between man's intelligence and the intuition of the animal.

Actually London wrote two versions of this story. Under date of December 22, 1908, London wrote to R. W. Gilder, editor of the *Century Magazine,* as follows:

> ...Somewhere in that mountain of letters is a bunch of correspondence relating "To Build a Fire." I cannot find it, and shall have to go on memory.
>
> A long, long time ago I wrote a story for boys which I sold to the *Youth's Companion.* It was purely juvenile in treatment; its motif was not only very strong, but very true. Man

> after man in the Klondike has died alone after getting his feet wet, through failure to build a fire. As years went by, I was worried about the inadequate treatment I had given that motif, and by the fact that I had treated it for boys merely. At last I came to the resolve to take the same motif and handle it for men. I had no access to the boys' version of it, and I wrote it just as though I had never used the motif before. I do not remember anything about the way I handled it for juveniles, but I do know, I am absolutely confident, that beyond the motif itself, there is no similarity of treatment whatever.
>
> I can only say that it never entered my head that there was anything ethically wrong in handling the same motif over again in the way I did, and I can only add that I am of the same opinion now, upon carefully considering the question. Please let me know how you feel about the matter.

The situation was that he had written "To Build a Fire" and published it on May 29, 1902, in the *Youth's Companion.* It is a very brief story and has little resemblance to the story that he published in the *Century Magazine* in 1908. He wrote the first version while he was in California. He wrote the second version while he was on the cruise of the *Snark.* And, therefore, did not have access to his former notes.

In the first version he has a man by the name of Tom Vincent set out alone on a trip in the Klondike. Vincent had heard the warning "never travel alone," but he paid no attention. He laughed at it because he was proud of his own strength. It was a bleak, dreary day; 60 degrees below zero. He had 30 miles of lonely trail to cover when he left Calumet Camp on the Yukon with a light pack to go up Ball Creek to the divide between it and Cherry Creek where his party was prospecting and hunting moose. As he walked he tried to avoid stepping into springs or getting his feet wet, but inadvertently he did. When he tried to build a fire, he noticed that his hands quickly chilled when he took off the mittens and he could not handle the matches. He tried to build a fire under a tree,

> but at the moment he was adding the first twigs to the fire a grievous thing happened: the pine boughs above his head were burdened with 4 months of snowfall and so finely adjusted were the burdens that his slight movement in collecting the twigs had been sufficient to disturb the balance.

After he had started the fire, the snow was dislodged from the boughs and fell on Tom Vincent's head and shoulders and blotted out the fire.

He attempted to build another fire, but this time away from the trees so that it could not be doused by the falling snow. But he found his fingers and hands too cold to gather the twigs and to light the match. He became desperate and felt that he must move on.

He started to hurry up the trail, but he could not run with wet feet at 60 below zero. He came to a sharp turn in the creek where he could look ahead for a mile, and realized that there was no sign of help in the white silence beyond.

Then his eyes chanced upon a high water lodgement of twigs and leaves and branches. If he could strike a match he could build a fire. He sat down awkwardly, began to plan his course by carefully lighting the matches against his trousers.

Time and again, thus holding both his hands, he scratched a bunch on his pant leg, and finally ignited it. But the flame burned into the flesh of his hands, and he involuntarily relaxed his hold and the bunch fell into the snow. While he tried vainly to pick it up it sizzled and went out. But he kept on trying. Then he remembered that somewhere, not far away, there was a moose hunter's cabin. If he could get to that he could be saved. So he started out again. He came upon it but found it deserted, and began to despair.

> He sank down, sobbing. All was over. In an hour at best, in that terrific temperature, he would be an icy corpse. But the love of life was strong in him, and he sprang again to his feet. He was thinking quickly. What if the matches did burn his hands? Burned hands were better than dead hands. No hands at all were better than death.

He continued to flounder along the trail and soon came upon another high water lodgement. There were twigs and branches and leaves and grasses, all dry and waiting for fire. And these he succeeded in setting aflame. Then he took off his pack, got out dry socks, dried his feet in front of the fire, and spent the night before the fire getting warm.

The next day he limped pitifully into the camp at the Cherry Creek divide, and in a month's time he was about on his feet and so lived.

There are several interesting features about this story. It was written very early in London's career, sometime before December of 1901. According to his Journal record, he submitted it for publication in December 1901. Consequently, it was written during London's period of financial depression, when he was frequently in the depths of despair. In many of London's Northland stories he does not name his characters as such, particularly into the second version of "To Build a Fire." But perhaps the most interesting element was the theme of "Love of Life." It is a theme that occurs again and again in London's writings. Tom Vincent was saved by his determination to live. It is perhaps this element that interested the editors of *Youth's Companion.* This is one of the few stories that was sold the first time it was submitted.

The second version of "To Build a Fire" was written aboard the *Snark* in the South Seas in 1908. It is curious that aboard a small boat and in the heat and turmoil of the South Seas London would turn back to the North and write so vivid a story of a Northland tragedy and Northland irony. In this version the man is unnamed.

He was a newcomer, and consequently the white silence of the Yukon made no impression upon him.

> The trouble with him was that he was without imagination. He was quick and alert in the things of life, but only in the things and not in the significances. Fifty degrees below zero meant eighty-odd degrees of frost. Such fact impressed him as being cold and uncomfortable and that was all. It did not lead him to meditate upon his frailty as a creature of temperature and upon man's frailty in general, able only to live within certain limits of heat and cold, and from there on it did not lead him to the conjectural field of immortality and men's place in the universe.

He was prepared for the cold with his mittens and his moccasins, and with ear flaps and with a heavy coat and though he speculated upon the cold and found that as he spat upon the ground the spittle crackled in the air, he was unconcerned. Along with this man, and this is a difference from the first story, there trotted a big native husky wolf dog.

> The animal was depressed by the tremendous cold. It knew that it was no time for travelling. Its instinct told it a truer tale than was told to the man by the man's judgment. In reality, it was not merely colder than fifty below zero; it was colder than sixty below, than seventy below. It was seventy-five below zero. Since the freezing-point is thirty-two above zero, it meant that one hundred and seven degrees of frost obtained.

The dog knew nothing about thermometers and possibly in its brain could not make a sharp distinction between 107 degrees below freezing and 101. But the dog had learned to burrow under the snow and cuddle in the warmth of it away from the air. It also had learned to appreciate fire.

As the man walked along the trail he contemplated the time of his arrival at the camp. He knew that if he maintained a certain speed he would be at Henderson Creek by 6 o'clock and would be with the boys.

He was careful as he walked on the trail not to step on certain places where the ice had barely frozen over, where he could break through and wet his feet. He knew that wetting his feet could be very dangerous. He avoided the hidden pools by noting a certain false appearance to the snow. Once he forced the dog to act as a trail breaker for him and found that the dog broke through. And after the dog had broken through by instinct it licked its legs and toes so that the ice could not form.

At mid-day the man built a fire, ate a lunch that he had carried under his coat, next to his body, and took time by the warmth of the fire to fill his pipe and have a comfortable smoke. And then he turned back to the trail. The dog was disappointed; he wanted to stay by the fire.

> This man did not know cold. Possibly all the generations of his ancestry had been ignorant of cold, of real cold, of cold one hundred and seven degrees below freezing point. But the dog knew; all its ancestry knew, and it had inherited the knowledge. And it knew that it was not good to walk abroad in such fearful cold.

During the afternoon the man inadvertently stepped on thin ice and found himself floundering in water, with his feet wet up to his knees. He knew the danger and knew that he must stop, build a fire and dry his feet and put on dry socks. He was able to start it with small twigs. He fed it very carefully.

> Gradually, as the flame grew stronger, he increased the size of the twigs with which he fed it. He squatted in the snow, pulling the twigs out from their entanglement in the brush and feeding directly to the flame. He knew there must be no failure.

Finally he felt that he was safe. The fire had been a success. The old timer had been serious in his statement that no man must travel alone in the Klondike after 50 below. Well, here he was. He had the accident, he was alone, he had kindled a fire and would save himself.

And then the unexpected happened. He had built the fire under a spruce tree which was weighted down with snow for many months, and when he pulled the twigs from the base of the tree he began an agitation, an imperceptable agitation, but enough to disturb the snow balance and bring about disaster. The snow fell from the tree upon the man and the fire, and the fire was blotted out.

With the fire gone, the man attempted to move along the trail but realized that he could not travel and attempted to build another fire. He was unsuccessful. He remembered the tale of a man caught in a blizzard who killed a steer and crawled inside the carcass and was so saved. He thought that he might kill the dog and thereby save his life. But when he spoke to the dog there was a strange note in his voice, and the dog was frightened and kept away from him. Then he tried to take to the trail again, but became weary and sat down.

Then the man drowsed off into what seemed to him the most comfortable and satisfying sleep he had ever known. The dog sat facing him and waiting. The brief day drew to a close in a long slow twilight. There were no signs of a fire to be made. Never in the dog's experience had it known a man to sit like that in the snow and make no fire. As the twilight drew on, its eager yearning for the fire mastered it, and with great shifting and lifting of its forefeet it whined softly then flattened its ears down in anticipation of being chidden by the man, but the man remained silent. Later the dog whined loudly and still later it crept close to the man and caught the scent of death. This made the animal bristle and back away. A little longer it delayed, howling under the stars that leaped and danced and shone brightly in the sky. Then it turned and trotted up the trail in the direction of the camp. It knew where to find other providers of food and fire.

It is the basic irony of life that man, with his knowledge, with his ability to clothe himself, to build a fire, to create warmth or to provide cold, could not survive in the Artic weather of 75 degrees below zero while the dog, living only on his instinct, without mittens, without ear flaps, without a coat, without lunch, and without a fire, saved himself.

In this story, as in the first version of the story and also in the story of "Love of Life," and again as reflected in "The Chinago," there is the permanent theme of man's desire to live. In the "Love of Life" it is the driving force that saves the man, but in "To Build a Fire," even with all the driving force it has, man cannot overcome the elements. The irony is that with all of his knowledge he is still a helpless victim to natural powers and natural forces.

Jack London loved life and he lived it as fully and as completely as any man. He admired men who cling or have clung to life in times of adversity. The love of life is a theme that runs through many of his novels and short stories. It is the theme of man enduring unbelievable suffering and hardship but tenaciously clinging to life.

Two of his best short stories were built around this theme; "To Build a Fire" and "Love of Life." In these stories men, alone in the vastness of the Northland, struggle against freezing cold, sometimes 75 degrees below zero, and endure unbelievable misery because of their will to live. In the first story the man fails and freezes to death. In the second story he succeeds and survives.

London wrote "Love of Life" early in 1903. He submitted it to the editor of *Cosmopolitan* who rejected it; to the editor of *Outing* who rejected it; and to the editor of *McClures* who accepted it and paid him $400. It was published in December 1905.

London, by this time, had established an international reputation. According to his records book it was sold again to *Blackwoods* Magazine that same month for 20 pounds or approximately $100. He also sold the French translation rights to *L'illustration* for $29.60 plus a 2 years' subscription to that magazine.

In "Love of Life," two men started out cross-country to the sea in hopes to catch a boat for the States. They each carried packs with their necessary food and clothing. Each had a moosehide sack containing gold bullion. Shortly after they had begun their journey in the extremely cold weather, one of them slipped and sprained his ankle. He called to the other, "I say Bill, I've sprained my ankle." Bill paid no attention. He staggered on through the cold leaving his companion behind, despite the pleas of the crippled man. After a short struggle the man was able to bind up his ankle and hobble painfully on. A few days later he attempted to shoot a young caribou only to find that his rifle had no ammunition.

In his wandering he lost his gun and his knife, so was weaponless. He struggled on, day after day, with his damaged ankle and without food, becoming weaker and weaker. Once, to lighten his load, he poured out part of the gold from the moose-hide sack; later he poured out the remainder.

Now and again the wolves, in packs of two and three, crossed his path. But they steered clear of him. They were not in sufficient numbers. Besides, they were hunting the caribou which did not battle, while this strange creature that walked erect might scratch and bite.

> One late afternoon he came upon scattered bones where the wolves had made a kill. The debris had been a caribou calf an hour before, squawking and running and very much alive. He contemplated the bones, clean-picked and polished, pink with the cell-life in them which had not yet died. Could it possibly be that he might be that ere the day was done! Such was life, eh? A vain and fleeting thing. It was only life that pained. There was no hurt in death. To die was to sleep. It meant cessation, rest. Then why was he not content to die?
>
> Came frightful days of snow and rain. He did not know when he made camp, when he broke camp. He travelled in the night as much as in the day. He rested wherever he fell, crawled on whenever the dying life in him flickered up and burned less dimly. He, as a man, no longer strove. It was the life in him, unwilling to die, that drove him on. He did not suffer. His nerves had become blunted, numb, while his mind was filled with wierd visions and delicious dreams.

One afternoon the man came upon a trail of another man, one who did not walk but crawled on all fours. He followed the trail of the other man who dragged himself along, and soon came to the end of it—a few fresh-picked bones upon a soggy mass marked by the foot-pads of many wolves.

> He saw a squat moose-hide sack, mate to his own, which had been torn by sharp teeth. He picked it up, though its weight was almost too much for his feeble fingers. Bill had carried it

> to the last. Ha! Ha! He would have the laugh on Bill. He would survive and carry it to the ship in the shining sea. His mirth was hoarse and ghastly, like a raven's croak, and a sick wolf joined him, howling lugubriously. The man ceased suddenly. How could he have the laugh on Bill if that were Bill; if those bones, so pinky-white and clean, were Bill?
>
> He turned away. Well, Bill had deserted him; but he would not take the gold, nor would he suck Bill's bones. Bill would have, though, had it been the other way around, he mused as he staggered on.

Here is real irony, a case of poetic justice, where retribution come to "Bill," and his bones are found by the injured man he had deserted.

A day or two before he found Bill's bones he had come into view of the sea and had sighted a ship, he thought a whaler, lying at anchor. The hope of reaching it gave him renewed courage. But his strength was almost gone and he knew that he was being followed by the sick wolf.

> The patience of the wolf was terrible. The man's patience was no less terrible. For half a day he lay motionless, fighting off unconsciousness and waiting for the thing that was to feed upon him and upon which he wished to feed.
>
> Sometimes the languid sea rose over him and he dreamed long dreams; but ever through it all, waking and dreaming, he waited for the wheezing breath and the harsh caress of the tongue.
>
> He did not hear the breath, and he slipped slowly from some dream to the feel of the tongue along his hand. He waited, the fangs pressed softly; the pressure increased; the wolf was exerting its last strength in an effort to sink teeth in the food for which it had waited so long. But the man had waited long, and the lacerated hand closed on the jaw. Slowly, while the wolf struggled feebly and the hand clutched feebly, the other hand crept across to a grip. Five minutes later the whole weight of the man's body was on top of the wolf. The hands had not sufficient strength to choke the wolf, but the face of the man was pressed close to the throat of the wolf and the mouth of the man was full of hair. At the end of half an hour the man was aware of a warm trickle in his throat. It was not pleasant. It was like molten lead being forced into his stomach, and it was forced by his will alone. Later the man rolled over on his back and slept.

It had been a contest between a dying man and a dying animal. Whichever first reached helpless exhaustion would be the other's victim. But the love of life was strong in the man and he won.

On board the whaler in the bay were some members of a scientific expedition. One day they noticed a strange object on the beach. They went ashore to investigate.

> They saw something that was alive but which would hardly be called a man. It was blind, unconscious. It squirmed along the ground like some monstrous worm. Most of its efforts were ineffectual, but it was persistent, and it writhed and twisted and went ahead perhaps a score of feet an hour.

The scientists took him aboard and nursed him back to health. Now comes the final touch of irony—he became obsessed with the fear that the food would not last and ate to the point of obesity. The fear of hunger drove him to obtain food by any means he could devise and when the scientist realized that his health was endangered by his overweight, they searched his bunk and found it lined with hardtack; the mattress was stuffed with hardtack; every nook and cranny was filled with hardtack. Yet he was sane. He was simply taking precautions against another famine.

So, ironically, the man whose love of life carried him through cold, exhaustion and starvation would have destroyed himself with food and inactivity had not the scientists interfered.

One of Jack London's most poetic stories is "The Law of Life." It is almost a picture poem, and yet it is a story in which he reveals, as much as in any other story, the depth of human tragedy. It was written early in 1900, and first submitted to the editor of the *Atlantic Monthly* who rejected it. He then submitted it to the editor of *McClures Magazine,* who accepted it and paid him $55; two cents a word. Later London frequently made 15 cents, 20 cents, and sometimes 25 cents a word.

"The Law of Life" is a story of an old Indian, apparently once a chief. His name was Koskoosh. The story opens;

> Old Koskoosh listened greedily. Though his sight had long since faded, his hearing was still acute, and the slightest sound penetrated to the glimmering intelligence which yet abode behind the withered forehead, but which no longer gazed forth upon the things of the world. Ah! that was Sit-cum-to-ha, shrilly anathematizing the dogs as she cuffed and beat them into the harnesses. Sit-cum-to-ha was his daughter's daughter, but she was too busy to waste a thought upon her broken grandfather, sitting alone there in the snow, forlorn and helpless. Camp must be broken. The long trail waited while the short day refused to linger. Life called her, and the duties of life, not death. And he was very close to death now.

Old Koskoosh sat by a small fire, living pretty much in the memories of his past. He remembered when he and a companion followed the trail of wolves which had separated an old moose from the herd and baited him and tormented him until they were able to kill and devour him.

The memories of this scene were very vivid in his mind, because now he was sitting by the fire and in a little while, at best a few short hours, his tribe would move away and leave him there to freeze to death or to be devoured by the wolves. But the tribe could not take him with them. It was necessary for them to find new hunting grounds, to find food and a warmer winter climate. They were loaded with the necessary tents, clothing and what food they had.

Even though he was the father of the chief of the tribe, he could not be taken, he must be discarded. So it was arranged that Sit-cum-to-ha would put wood beside him so that he could keep the fire going at least for a few short hours and thus keep the wolves away.

He could hear them moving camp and knew that in a little while he would be left to die, but that was nature.

> But one task did Nature set the individual. Did he not perform it, he died. Did he perform it, it was all the same, he died. Nature did not care; there were plenty who were obedient, and it was only the obedience in this matter, not the obedient, which lived and lived always. The tribe of Koskoosh was very old. The old men he had known when a boy, had known old men before them. Therefore it was true that the tribe lived, that it stood for the obedience of all its members, way down into the forgotten past, whose very restingplaces were unremembered. They did not count; they were episodes. They had passed away like clouds from a summer sky. He also was an episode, and would pass away. Nature did not care.

And as he mused, the tribe got ready to go, but before it left his son came and placed his hand upon his shoulder and bade him good-by. This touched the old man. His son was very kind to take a moment to say good-by to him before they left. Then they were gone.

He could see around the fringe of the fire the gathering of the wolves. He knew that as soon as the fire failed the wolves would close in and devour him. He felt a cold muzzle thrust against his cheek, and he rebelled against it. He took a burning fagot from the fire and pushed it toward the beast. The brute withdrew but the other wolves around howled and panted and snarled at him.

> Now one wormed his chest forward, dragging his haunches after, now a second, now a third; but never a one drew back. Why should he cling to life? he asked, and dropped the blazing stick into the snow. It sizzled and went out. The circle grunted uneasily but held its own. Again he saw the last stand of the old bull moose, and Koskoosh dropped his head wearily upon his knees. What did it matter after all? Was it not the law of life?

London was well aware of this "law" operating in his own

time, when industry and professions alike discarded men who were no longer productive. In the days before Social Security and pension plans, men who became too old or decrepit to work were a burden to the family or the tribe, and the tribe or family often discarded them. Perhaps the bitterest irony of all is that such should be "The Law of Life."

I said earlier that most critics consider "To Build a Fire" as London's greatest. My choice, however, is "The Chinago." I believe, from the point of view of the building of an atmosphere, the telling of a narrative, and the development of irony, that "The Chinago" is the greatest story of London's career and one of the great stories of all time.

It was written while he was on the cruise of the *Snark* in the South Seas in 1909. He submitted it to the following magazines—*Colliers Weekly, Everybody's, Success, Cosmopolitan, American Magazine, Women's Home Companion, McClures, Century, Outing, Saturday Evening Post*—all of which rejected it. It was accepted by *Harpers* and published in July, 1909 and in an English magazine in September, 1909. *Harpers* paid him $500 and he received approximately $100 from the English publication.

"Chinago" was a term applied by the Tahitians to the Chinese coolies who were indentured and brought to the islands as laborers for the plantations, but who were, in reality, slaves. By the terms of the indenture the coolie was signed to a period of servitude, usually 5 years. He was paid 50 cents per day. There were men in the Chinese villages who worked for $10, $5, or even $4 a year. So the Chinago considered himself lucky to have the opportunity to work for 50 cents a day—and for 5 years.

Ah Cho was one of these Chinagos. He worked on a plantation for an English company in Tahiti along with 500 other Chinagos. One night one Chinago, Ah San, murdered another Chinago, Chung Ga. Five Chinagos witnessed the killing and were found by the overseer, Schemmer, in the room with the body of Chung Ga, but Ah San had escaped. All 498 Chinagos knew that Ah San was the killer, but they had secretly agreed never to betray another Chinago. The French court tried the five men who were taken by Schemmer at the time of the murder.

Ah Cho listened to the trial. He was complacent because he believed that justice would be done and that a man innocent of the crime would not be convicted. He did not understand the courtroom arguments, which were held in French, and he could not understand why the Frenchmen were so stupid as to not be able to find out who killed Chung Ga.

> So it was that Ah Cho reasoned, when he, along with his four companions, had lied and blocked and obfuscated in their statements to the court concerning what had taken place. They had heard the sounds of the killing, and, like Schemmer, they had run to the spot. They had got there before Schemmer—that was all. True, Schemmer had testified that, attracted by the sounds of the quarreling as he chanced to pass by, he had stood for at least five minutes outside; and then, when he entered, he found the prisoners already inside; and that they had not entered just before, because he had been standing by the only door to the barracks. But what of that? Ah Cho and his four fellow-prisoners had testified that Schemmer was mistaken. In the end they would be let go. They were all confident of that. Five men could not have their heads cut off for two stab wounds. Besides, no foreign devil had seen the killing. But these Frenchmen were so stupid. In China, as Ah Cho well knew, the magistrate would order all of them to the torture and learn the truth. The truth was very easy to learn under torture. But these Frenchmen did not torture, bigger fools they! Therefore they would never find out who killed Chung Ga.

It was evident that the one thing the court must do was to find one man guilty and execute him. It must also establish degrees of guilt among the other four for various degrees of punishment. This must be done for exemplary reasons.

When the court handed down the decision, Ah Chow was found guilty of murder and sentenced to death; Ah Cho, second in guilt was sentenced to 20 years imprisonment at Caledonia.

Ah Cho all during the trial had dreamed of completing his indenture and returning to China where, with his savings, he could buy him a small home, rear a family, and live out his life in comfort. He had already served 3 years of the indenture, had 2 more to go, and was 22 years old. Even as he heard the sentence he was not too disturbed because he could wait another 20 years and he would still have time to return to his native land and live in his beloved garden.

> The five Chinagos were taken back to jail. They were not shocked nor grieved. The sentences being unexpected was quite what they were accustomed to in their dealings with the white devils. From them a Chinago rarely expected more than the unexpected. The heavy punishment for a crime they had not committed was no stranger than the countless strange things that white devils did. In the weeks that followed, Ah Cho often contemplated Ah Chow with mild curiosity. His head was to be cut off by the guillotine that was being erected on the plantation. For him there would be no declining years, no gardens of tranquility. Ah Cho philosophized and speculated about life and death. As for himself, he was not perturbed. Twenty years were merely twenty years. By that much was

> his garden removed from him—that was all. He was young, and the patience of Asia was in his bones. He could wait those twenty years, and by that time the heats of his blood would be assuaged and he would be better fitted for that garden of calm delight. He though of a name for it; he would call it The Garden of the Morning Calm. He was made happy all day by the thought, and he was inspired to devise a moral maxim on the virtue of patience.

And then one morning Cruchot, a gendarme, went to the chief justice to pick up the order commanding the jailer to give up the person of Ah Chow for execution.

> Now, it happened that the Chief Justice had given a dinner the night before to the captain and officers of the French man-of-war. His hand was shaking when he wrote out the order, and his eyes were aching so dreadfully that he did not read over the order. It was only a Chinago's life he was signing away, anyway. So he did not notice that he had omitted the final letter in Ah Chow's name. The order read "Ah Cho," and, when Cruchot presented the order, the jailer turned over to him the person of Ah Cho.

Cruchot took Ah Cho in the wagon beside him behind two mules and drove away. Ah Cho thought that he was going back to the plantation and he beamed at the gendarme. Finally the gendarme said to him, "You are funny," and Ah Cho beamed more ardently.

> "I am glad to get out of the jail."
> "Is that all?" The gendarme shrugged his shoulder.
> "Is it not enough?" was the retort.
> "Then you are glad to have your head cut off?"
> Ah Cho looked at him in abrupt perplexity and said:—"Why I am going back to Atimaono to work on the plantation for Schemmer. Are you not taking me to Atimaono?"

Ah Cho was alarmed but still had faith that justice would prevail and that before they guillotined him they would rectify the mistake in the spelling of his name. But the gendarme, after 20 years of experience, knew all too well not to question the order of a superior and he would deliver Ah Cho to the executioner even though he was aware of the error.

> So the time passed nicely until Atimaono was reached and the mules trotted up to the foot of the scaffold, in the shade of which stood the impatient sergeant. Ah Cho was hurried up the ladder of the scaffold. Beneath him on one side he saw assembled all the coolies of the plantation. Schemmer had decided that the event would be a good object lesson, and so had called in the coolies from the fields and compelled them to be present. As they caught sight of Ah Cho they gabbled among themselves in low voices. They saw the mistake; but

> they kept it to themselves. The inexplicable white devils had doubtlessly changed their minds. Instead of taking the life of one innocent man, they were taking the life of another innocent man. Ah Chow or Ah Cho—what did it matter which?

Schemmer was the executioner. He had built the guillotine himself. When Ah Cho was turned over to Schemmer he explained that there had been an error. Schemmer was surprised. He swore tersely for a few seconds, and looked regretfully across at the thing he had made with his own hands. He was eager to see it work.

> "Look here," he said finally, "we can't postpone this affair. I've lost three hours' work already out of those five hundred Chinagos. I can't afford to lose it all over again for the right man. Let's put the performance through just the same. It is only a Chinago."

And so, Ah Cho, who had no guilt, learned in a few brief moments that all of his dreams and hopes would be destroyed by a spelling mistake made by a drunken judge, to whom it did not matter. He learned that justice is a convenience to be used by some men for mastery over other men; that human life is but a pawn to be created and destroyed according to the whims of fate. Such was the diabolical irony in the case of Ah Cho, "just another Chinago."

These are but four examples selected from approximately 150 stories. All of the 150 are not masterpieces but many are, and those that are will live and find a place in the permanent literature of the world. They testify to the genius of Jack London, master of irony and master craftsman of the short story.

Jack London's Symbolic Wilderness: Four Versions

EARLE LABOR

Any reader of London is aware of the wilderness as a pervading symbol in his works. In this essay Professor Labor notes that the wilderness assumed many forms and symbolic functions in London's writings. The symbol is important not only because of its function in the works but also because by looking at it we can trace London's attitude toward the American Dream. Such a view helps us see a development in London's works and to see London vis-a-vis other critics of that Dream.

In a recent article[1] Gordon Mills has indicated "the symbolic wilderness" as a motif that links Jack London with the well-known host of nineteenth-century romantic primitivists led by James Fenimore Cooper. Despite the strength of this motif and its persistence in London's fiction, however, Mills finds its varying applications confused, contradictory, even insincere at times. I wish to suggest, on the contrary, that a close reading of London's works reveals neither his confusion nor his lack of sincerity so much as his remarkable tact in handling complex symbolic patterns. The oversight in Mills's essay derives from his failure to realize that there are at least four separate versions of the symbolic wilderness in London's fiction—not merely one—and that each version is endowed with its own special qualities.

The first of these four versions is the White Silence, the vast, still wilderness of the Northland. Here, nature is cold, austere, and inviolable; man, puny and insignificant. As London explains,

[1]"The Symbolic Wilderness: James Fenimore Cooper and Jack London," *NCF*, XIII (March, 1959), 329-340.

> Nature has many tricks wherewith she convinces man of his finity,—the ceaseless flow of the tides, the fury of the storm, the shock of the earthquake, the long roll of heaven's artillery,—but the most tremendous, the most stupefying of all, is the passive phase of the White Silence. All movement ceases, the sky clears, the heavens are as brass; the slightest whisper seems sacrilege, and man becomes timid, affrighted at the sound of his own voice. Sole speck of life journeying across the ghostly wastes of a dead world, he trembles at his audacity, realizes that his is a maggot's life, nothing more. Strange thoughts arise unsummoned, and the mystery of all things strives for utterance. And the fear of death, of God, of the universe, comes over him,—the hope of the Resurrection and the Life, the yearning for immortality, the vain striving of the imprisoned essence,—it is then, if ever, man walks alone with God.[2]

The northern wilderness is, in one sense, a "wasteland," as Mills calls it; yet it is not without a stern moral influence. The god of the White Silence is a harsh god but a just one: he is an inflexible disciplinarian who brooks no violation of his strict code. He is "indifferent" in that he neither helps nor actively hinders man in this creature's petty enterprises, nor do these enterprises appreciably alter the wilderness. On the other hand, man himself, in order to survive, must be altered; and this alteration is for the better, morally speaking, because it calls forth such virtues as courage, integrity, and brotherhood:

> ...in the young Northland, frosty and grim and menacing, men stripped off the sloth of the south and gave battle greatly. And they stripped likewise much of the veneer of civilization—all of its follies, most of its foibles, and perhaps a few of its virtues....but they reserved the great traditions and at least lived frankly, laughed honestly and looked one another in the eyes.[3]

In book after book London stresses the importance of moral as well as physical adaptability for those who endure the rigors of the White Silence:

> The man who turns his back upon the comforts of an elder civilization, to face the savage youth, the primordial simplicity of the North, may estimate his success at an inverse ratio to the quantity and quality of his hopelessly fixed habits. He will soon discover, if he be a fit candidate, that the material habits are the less important.... his pinch will come in learning properly to shape his mind's attitude toward all things, and especially toward his fellow man. For the courtesies of ordinary life, he must substitute unselfishness, forbearance, and toler-

[2]"The White Silence," *The Son of the Wolf* (New York, 1900), p. 7.

[3]*A Daughter of the Snows* (New York, 1902), p. 202.

> ance. Thus, and thus only, can he gain that pearl of great price, —true comradeship.[4]

With all this in its favor, however, the northern wilderness is not a satisfactory Eden. It is a place of frightening purity and simplicity; although a source of moral and spiritual purgation, it provides neither warmth nor security. It is a region to escape FROM—not TO. Nature here is inimical to life. Man may find a certain serenity in the arctic wastes, but it is the blank serenity of death. Nowhere does London convey this idea more effectively than in the opening description of setting in *White Fang*:

> A vast silence reigned over the land. The land itself was a desolation, lifeless, without movement, so lone and cold that the spirit of it was not even that of sadness. There was a hint in it of laughter, but of a laughter more terrible than any sadness.... It was the masterful and incommunicable wisdom of eternity laughing at the futility of life and the effort of life. It was the Wild, the savage, frozen-hearted Northland Wild.[5]

The spirit of this wilderness is not, to be sure, the same spirit that hovers benevolently over Leatherstocking's forest—nor was it meant to be. It is the awesome naturalistic genie invoked by Darwin and Haeckel, and celebrated by Stephen Crane and Theodore Dreiser as well as by London. Under its domain men are no more than "specks and motes, moving with weak cunning and little wisdom amidst the play and interplay of the great blind elements and forces" (pp. 5-6).

Failing to discover his paradise in the northern wilderness, London looked to the tropics. Here we encounter two versions of his symbolic wilderness: Melanesia and Polynesia. Melanesia is London's Inferno. Contrasting with the cold purity of the White Silence, the Melanesian jungles are hot, putrid, and malign. We need only to compare London's writings about the Solomon Islands with his Alaskan tales to perceive the distinct symbolic values attributed to each version. Most noteworthy is the difference of moral influence. Though the Northland traveler may be caught amidst the "interplay of the great blind elements and forces," a certain cosmic orderliness nevertheless prevails in the harsh, immutable laws of this wilderness. Those who survive are made better because of their adaptation to its laws; those who are weak in physical or moral character do not survive. This is the Darwinian ethic at its finest. Men are drawn together in a closer bond of sympathy and brotherhood because such qualities are essential to survival, as are courage, honesty,

[4] "In a Far Country," *The Son of the Wolf*, pp. 69-70.

[5] *White Fang* (New York, 1906), p. 3.

and selflessness. The outer cold of the arctic world stimulates an inner warmth of companionship among the men who brave its hardships. And always the stern, terrible god of the White Silence is present to punish and correct those who violate his code. Finally, the man who is to endure the long arctic winter must be exceptionally gifted in that highest of human faculties—imagination: he must understand the ways of the Northland so sympathetically that he can anticipate its emergencies before they occur, always adapting himself to nature's laws, never attempting foolishly to impose the frail, devious customs of society and civilization upon the inviolable wilderness.

Such is not the case with Melanesia. Here the Darwinian law operates in its most insidious forms: dysentery, malaria, and loathsome skin diseases attack the good and the bad alike without respect for bravery, integrity, or imagination—the air itself "is saturated with a poison," London tells us, and "many strong men who escape dying there return as wrecks to their own countries."[6] This, rather than the Northland, is the real waste land of London's fiction. In Melanesia the concept of the wilderness as Eden is inverted: the Melanesian god is the Prince of Blackness himself, and his myrmidons are the cannibalistic natives whose

> highest instinct of sportsmanship is to catch a man with his back turned and to smite him a cunning blow with a tomahawk that severs the spinal column at the base of the brain. ... on some islands, such as Malaita, the profit and loss account of social intercourse is calculated in homicides. Heads are a medium of exchange, and white heads are extremely valuable.[7]

Instead of bringing out the best in those who survive, Melanesia brings out the worst; especially is this true of the white man. Those qualities which were spiritual assets in the Northland—comradeship and imagination, for example—become liabilities here. To live in the Solomons, the white man must have "a certain colossal self-satisfaction, and a racial egotism that convinces him that one white is better than a thousand niggers every day in the week, and that on Sunday he is able to clean out two thousand niggers"; furthermore, he "must not understand too well the instincts, customs, and mental processes of the blacks, the yellows, and the browns; for it is not in such fashion that the white race has tramped its royal road around the world" (pp. 200-201). The Melanesian wilderness is the

[6] "The Terrible Solomons," *South Sea Tales* (Tower Books Edition: New York, 1946), p. 199.

[7] *Ibid.*, pp. 199-200. London's Solomon Islanders appear to be identical—both symbolically and literally—to Poe's evil, black-toothed savages of the "Tsalemon" islands in *The Narrative of Arthur Gordon Pym*. In the story "Mauki" London explains how the natives' teeth are turned "lamp-black" by being compressed in a powdered mineral dug from a landslide on Malaita, "the most savage island in the Solomons" (p. 84).

source of further corruption—not of purification. In the midst of ruthless savagery, the white man is reduced to like savagery; human values are cruelly subverted in this rotting green hell. The theme of dissolution, moral as well as physical, is central to London's Melanesian fiction. As one character cynically confesses, "I've been in the tropics too long. I'm a sick man, a damn sick man. And the whiskey, and the sun, and the fever have made me sick in morals, too. Nothing's too mean and low for me now, and I can understand why the niggers eat each other, and take heads, and such things. I could do it myself."[8] London expressed his own feelings about Melanesia unequivocally when he wrote, "If I were a king, the worst punishment I could inflict on my enemies would be to banish them to the Solomons. On second thought, king or no king, I don't think I'd have the heart to do it."[9]

In contrast, London loved the islands of Polynesia. With their fertile valleys and cool, flower-swept mountains, their golden youths and maidens, their salubrious climate, these islands would seem to be Eden itself. It is significant that London's autobiographic hero Martin Eden yearns for Polynesia when suffering from neurasthenic disillusionment.[10] And London himself makes the association of Polynesia with Elysium explicit in such lyrical passages as the following:

> As I write these lines I lift my eyes and look seaward. I am on the beach of Waikiki on the island of Oahu. Far, in the azure sky, the trade-wind clouds drift low over the blue-green turquoise of the deep sea. Nearer, the sea is emerald and light olive-green. Then comes the reef, where the water is all slaty purple flecked with red. Still nearer are brighter greens and tans, lying in alternate stripes and showing where sandbeds lie between the living coral banks. Through and over and out of these wonderful colors tumbles and thunders a magnificent surf. As I say, I lift my eyes to all this, and through the white crest of a breaker suddenly appears a dark figure, erect, a man-fish or a sea-god, on the very forward face of the crest.... It is a Kanaka on a surf-board. And I know that when I have finished these lines I shall be out in that riot of color and pounding surf, trying to hit those breakers even as he, and failing as he never failed, but living life as the best of us may live it. And the picture of that colored sea and that flying sea-god Kanaka becomes another reason for the young man to

[8] *A Son of the Sun* (New York, 1912), pp. 17-18.

[9] *The Cruise of the Snark* (New York, 1911), pp. 282-283.

[10] See *Martin Eden* (Rinehart Edition: New York, 1956), pp. 319-320. Note that, as his condition worsens, Martin's visions of the wilderness tend subtly to shift from Polynesia to Melanesia (see p. 359).

> go west, and farther west, beyond the Baths of Sunset, and still west till he arrives home again.[11]

With all this loveliness, however, Polynesia is not the Eden it once was; it is, in reality, Paradise Lost, an Elysium despoiled by the inevitable white man. Unlike the god of the White Silence and the foul fiend of the Melanesian jungles, the god of Polynesia is a benevolent diety. He is neither impassive nor malignant but, unfortunately, he is weak. His tender beneficence extends to all men, both good and evil; he has no code except that of loving kindness and abundance for all. His wilderness is therefore defenseless against the unscrupulous advance of commercialism and civilization. In such stories as "Koolau the Leper" and "Shin Bones" London depicts the tragic despoliation of this wilderness by the materialistic Nordic. "This is the twentieth century, and we stink of gasoline," one character remarks;[12] and his insight foreshadows a dominant theme of modern literature. During his visit to Typee, London noted the contrast between the happy primitives described in Herman Melville's first novel and the miserable survivors of the twentieth century:

> Life has rotted away in this wonderful garden spot, where the climate is as delightful and healthful as any to be found in the world. Not alone were the Typeans physically magnificent; they were pure.... When one considers the situation, one is almost driven to the conclusion that the white race flourishes on impurity and corruption....[13]

Polynesia might have fulfilled London's dream of Eden, but he arrives there too late – the islands had already been found and violated.

In addition to the Northland, Melanesia, and Polynesia, there is yet a fourth version of the symbolic wilderness in London's fiction: the Valley of the Moon. Disenchanted with the northern wilds and the tropics, London focused his attention with increasing intensity upon the great virgin forests of the American West. Five novels—*White Fang* (1906), *Burning Daylight* (1910), *The Abysmal Brute* (1913), *The Valley of the Moon* (1913), and *The Little Lady of the Big House* (1916)—deal with this version. As we shall see, the American Eden differs in many ways from the Northland and the tropics; it also differs from the American wilderness as represented in the works of earlier writers such as Cooper, Farnham, and Webber.[14]

[11] *The Cruise of the Snark,* pp. 58-59.

[12] "Shin Bones," *On the Makaloa Mat* (New York, 1919), p. 141.

[13] *The Cruise of the Snark,* p. 170.

[14] See Henry Nash Smith, *Virgin Land* (Vintage Edition: New York, 1957), pp. 77ff.

Perhaps the main feature that distinguishes the Valley of the Moon from the other three versions of London's wilderness is this: only in this last version does London envision man as making a satisfactory long-term adjustment to natural surroundings. The central problem arising from this feature is how to place man in the wilderness, to enable him to live in nature and partake of its restorative essence without contaminating the crystal springs from which he drinks. The problem did not present itself in the other versions of wilderness: in the Northland those springs were frozen and in the tropics they were already polluted. But in the American West they were both accessible and pure, at least as London saw them. The attempt to place man harmoniously within nature involved several considerations, in making which London was neither confused nor insincere—but merely optimistic. First, the wilderness itself must be benevolent toward man; it must be both virginal and tractable. Second, man himself must be spiritually purified BEFORE entering the wilderness. Third, after undergoing a cleansing of the baser motives of civilization—after being reborn—man could impose social refinements and scientific methods upon nature, so long as these changes "improved" the wilderness without desecrating it. Finally, the initiate must become a self-appointed guardian of the wilderness, protecting it against all attempts to assault and corrupt morally or materialistically. As a result of these considerations, London's fiction about the American wilderness assumes qualities of the pastoral romance. Such an idyllic element is, for obvious reasons, generally alien to the fiction of the White Silence and the tropics.

London's first two novels presenting the American idyll contrast it dramatically with the northern wilderness. *White Fang* opens with one of London's finest descriptions of the vast, cold lifelessness of the arctic wastes; the controlling metaphors are those of toil, suffering, and death. The pastoral wilderness into which White Fang moves at the end of the novel is, on the other hand, a place of abundance, life, and movement:

> There was plenty of food and no work in the Southland, and White Fang lived fat and prosperous and happy. Not alone was he in the geographical Southland, for he was in the Southland of life. Human kindness was like a sun shining upon him, and he flourished like a flower planted in good soil.[15]

Here is the American Dream as Crèvecoeur had described it, an Edenic wilderness of boundless fertility and happiness. White Fang's new home is a far cry from the stark, primeval wilderness of the

[15] *White Fang*, p. 305.

Northland; it is a place of love and humanity. But its beauty and salubrity are not inviolable: they must be protected from evil invaders, represented in this case by Jim Hall, an escaped convict who sneaks onto Judge Scott's idyllic ranch to kill the man who sentenced him. White Fang proves his right to Edenic privileges by saving the judge's life, and is consequently christened "Blessed Wolf." Having proved himself worthy of his new environment, the dog-hero settles into the Southland's softly modulated rhythms: and the novel concludes with White Fang drowsing comfortably in the life-giving California sun, while his new-born puppies romp around him.

The Northland-Southland polarity also provides the structural basis for *Burning Daylight.* But this novel, unlike *White Fang,* places emphasis upon man's heroic stature rather than upon his puny insignificance amid the crushing forces of the White Silence. The central character is Elam Harnish, nicknamed "Burning Daylight" because of his rest-defying vitality. A true child of the wilderness, morally simple and pure, Harnish is one in whom the life force pulses so strongly that he is a match even for the "frozen hearted Northland Wild": "Desire for mastery was strong in him, and it was all one whether wrestling with the elements themselves, with men, or with luck in the gambling game.... It was the urge of Life healthy and strong, unaware of frailty and decay, drunken and sublime complacence, ego-mad, enchanted by its own mighty optimism."[16] After accumulating a large fortune in gold, Elam leaves the Northland, seeking new adventures, particularly financial adventures, in the civilized Southland, which to his naïve eyes appears to be no more than "another kind of wilderness." He soon discovers that the jungle of big business is far more savage than the arctic wilds. Quickly mulcted of his eleven million dollars by a group of smooth-talking robber barons, Harnish abandons his sense of humanity and fair play in order to compete in this new environment.

Elam manages to recoup his fortune but, in doing so, undergoes a radical moral change:

> Power had its effect on him that it had on all men. Suspicious of the big exploiters, despising the fools of the exploited herd, he had faith only in himself. This led to an undue and erroneous exaltation of his ego, while kindly consideration of others—nay, even simple respect—was destroyed, until naught was left for him but to worship at the shrine of self (p. 180).

In the Northland Elam's egotistic strength was a heroic virtue, for it was necessitated and balanced by the awesome forces of nature.

[16] *Burning Daylight* (New York, 1910), p. 61.

These same forces pressed men together in a common bond of mutual aid and companionship; without this meliorating factor, however, strength degenerates into ruthless brutality and egotism grows cancerous—"Cities did not make for comradeship as did the Alaskan trail" (p. 274).

Only by renouncing his wealth and the corrupt life of the city may Harnish achieve his salvation. That such renunciation is a religious act London implies in his description of the pastoral wilderness itself; Elam's spiritual reformation begins with his first excursion into the Valley of the Moon:

> He halted his horse, for beside the spring uprose a wild California lily. It was a wonderful flower, growing there in the cathedral nave of lofty trees. At least eight feet in height, its stem rose straight and slender, green and bare, for two-thirds its length, and then burst into a shower of snow-white waxen bells. There were hundreds of these blossoms, all from the one stem, delicately poised and ethereally frail. Daylight had never seen anything like it. Slowly his gaze wandered from it to all that was about him. He took off his hat, with almost a vague religious feeling. This was different. No room for contempt and evil here. This was clean and fresh and beautiful—something he could respect. It was like a church. The atmosphere was one of holy calm. Here man felt the prompting of nobler things (p. 184).

His reformation is consummated by his love for Dede Mason, a displaced woodland spirit who works in Daylight's office. Like Rima of Hudson's *Green Mansions,* Dede serves as priestess-guide for Harnish in his return to the wilderness. Also, it is she who convinces Elam that he must give up his money if he is to gain salvation: "All these last years you have been living unnaturally," she tells him; "You, a man of the open, have been cooping yourself up in the cities with all that that means. You are not the same man at all, and your money is destroying you. You are becoming something different, something not so healthy, not so clean, not so nice. Your money and your way of life are doing it" (p. 292). Fully awakened to the pastoral beauties of the Valley of the Moon and to the corresponding elevation of Dede's love, Harnish finally renounces both his fortune and the city, and moves into the Valley of the Moon. His transformation, like White Fang's, reinforces Crèvecoeur's famous dictum that "Men are like plants; the goodness and flavour of the fruit proceeds from the peculiar soil and exposition in which they grow." London echoes these words in describing Daylight's new birth under the combined influences of love and the wilderness: "... he had been afraid of love all his life only in the end to come to find it the greatest thing in the world. Not alone were [Elam and Dede] well mated, but in coming to live on the ranch they had selected the best soil in which their love would prosper" (p. 350).

London's treatment of the wilderness theme in *The Abysmal Brute* and *The Valley of the Moon* is essentially the same as in *White Fang* and *Burning Daylight.* Pat Glendon, the hero of *The Abysmal Brute,* is a prize fighter who denounces the corruption of city life as manifested in the fight game and then retires with his new bride to the "pure" life of the California wilderness (again it is the woman who disabuses the hero concerning the evils of city living). Likewise, Billy Roberts—also a boxer—and Saxon Brown, the principals of *The Valley of the Moon,* find their salvation amid the healing elements of the Sonoma wilderness after their marriage has nearly collapsed in strike-ridden San Francisco. The city-wilderness antithesis is sharply delineated in Saxon's sad meditations after the stillbirth of her child and the jailing of her husband during the teamster strike:

> She sat there, racking her brain, the smudge of Oakland at her back, staring across the bay at the smudge of San Francisco. Yet the sun was good; the wind was good, as was the keen salt air in her nostrils; the blue sky, flecked with clouds, was good. All the natural world was right, and sensible, and beneficent. It was the man-world that was wrong, and mad, and horrible. Why were the stupid stupid? Was it a law of God? No; it could not be. God had made the wind, and air, and sun. The man-world was made by man, and a rotten job it was.[17]

But, like the Harnishes and the Glendons, Billy and Saxon recapture Eden in the Valley of the Moon; and, as in the case of White Fang, their rebirth is confirmed when they are christened "You blessed children" by Edmund Hale, the ancient priest of the Sonoma wilderness. The novel concludes with the further promise of new life in Saxon's announcement of her pregnancy as she and Billy, standing symbolically beside a quiet pool in the heart of their canyon, gaze serenely upon a doe and new-born fawn at the edge of the forest.

The Little Lady of the Big House concludes on an altogether different note. The last novel in which London dealt with the theme of the American Eden, *The Little Lady* reveals the collapse of his faith in the restorative powers of this wilderness. There is an unmistakably personal element in the novel: its central characters, Dick and Paula Forrest (note the symbolic surname), are in many ways identical to Jack and Charmian London; and their ranch closely resembles London's place at Glen Ellen, California. Unlike the other works of London's pastoral wilderness, *The Little Lady* is informed by a mood of

[17] *The Valley of the Moon* (New York, 1913), p. 254.

cynical irony. On the surface, the Forrests seem to be an ideally mated couple: they are both splendid physical specimens, dynamic, amiable, sensitive, fun-loving, intelligent, and very appreciative of each other's virtues. They live in a beautiful home enveloped in the love of friends and in the rich abundance of nature (Dick is a scientific breeder of prize stock). Yet, despite these outward signs of an almost Edenic bliss, something is obscurely amiss in the Forrest household: Paula is a chronic insomniac, Dick sleeps with a loaded .44 Colt's automatic at his bedside, and—most disturbing—their marriage is barren.

Because the Forrests themselves have no children, the theme of natural fecundity that runs through the novel assumes a pathological significance. Dick reiterates this theme obsessively in his favorite songs, such as "The Song of Mountain Lad" (the Forrests' prize stud):

> "Hear me! I am Eros. I stamp upon the hills. I fill the wide valleys. The mares hear me, and startle, in quiet pastures; for they know me. The grass grows rich and richer, the land is filled with fatness, and the sap is in the trees. It is the spring. The spring is mine. I am monarch of my kingdom of the spring."[18]

Though capable of fostering the abundance of nature, the Forrests are frustrated in their own most basic function as mates. Ostensibly their marriage is broken up by Evan Graham, Dick's best friend, who falls in love with Paula; but, more subtly, the breach has already been made by the Forrests' failure to become parents. Dick ponders suicide when he discovers his wife's attachment to Graham; before he can carry out his plan, however, Paula shoots herself. Her dying words to Dick are, "I'm sorry there were no babies, Red Cloud" (p. 391). The irony that has been merely hinted at earlier breaks through as harsh mockery in the novel's conclusion:

> After a long time, she sighed faintly, and began so easily to go that she was gone before they guessed. From without, the twittering of the canaries bathing in the fountain penetrated the silence of the room, and from afar came the trumpeting of Mountain Lad and the silver whinny of the Frothingham Princess (p. 392).

As London's final statement upon the American wilderness as Eden, *The Little Lady of the Big House* is a depressing and important book: an artistic failure, it was his last serious attempt at novel-writing; and it was published only a few months before his probable suicide.* In view of its contents, these hardly seem coincidences.

[18]*The Little Lady of the Big House* (New York, 1916), pp. 84-85.

**Author's Note:* My inference concerning London's "probable suicide" was drawn from Irving Stone's *Sailor on Horseback* (Boston: Houghton Mifflin, 1938), pp. 331-32. Since the pub-

London had run through several wildernesses in his quest for Elysium and, though frustrated by his essays into the Northland and the tropics, he had been sustained by the old American Dream. But in the end even this failed him—as it had failed Melville, Twain, and Henry Adams. Perhaps in this respect London's tragedy is America's tragedy as well. In any case, to say that he was insincere in his treatment of the Dream and that "the wilderness as a symbol placed in opposition to civilization must have little force in London's fiction," as Mills has suggested, is neither fair nor accurate. The seeming contradictions in London's portrayals of the symbolic wilderness are, in fact, consistent variations on the theme of progressive disillusionment. Considering the pressures under which London wrote, his tactful handling of the four versions of this wilderness is a rather impressive achievement.

---

lication of my essay in 1962, Stone's suicide canard has been discredited by several London scholars. See, for example, Alfred S. Shivers, "Jack London: Not a Suicide," *The Dalhousie Review,* 49 (Spring 1969), 43-57; Kevin Starr, *Americans and the California Dream* (New York: Oxford Univ. Press, 1973), p. 237; Earle Labor, *Jack London* (New York: Twayne, 1974), pp. 122-23; Clarice Stasz, "The Social Construction of Biography: The Case of Jack London," *Modern Fiction Studies,* 22 (Spring 1976), 66-67; Andrew Sinclair, *Jack: A Biography of Jack London* (New York: Harper & Row, 1977), pp. 232-42. Also, for a revision of my own interpretation of London's final attitude toward the American wilderness, see *Jack London,* pp. 136-46, and "From 'All Gold Canyon' to *The Acorn-Planter:* Jack London's Agrarian Vision," *Western American Literature,* 11 (Summer 1976), 83-101.

Jack London's Use of Carl Jung's *Psychology of the Unconscious*

JAMES I. McCLINTOCK

Throughout his writing career, London embraced various intellectual stances. Concepts which we can trace to Darwin, Spencer, and Marx are evident in many of the earlier works. Professor McClintock identifies another of London's perspectives, Jungian psychology, in On the Makaloa Mat. *Stories in this collection reveal London's use of archetypal myths attributed to Jung and Freud, myths which embrace such concepts as the libido (which represented to London the energy so evident in many of his characters), Oedipal myths, and symbolic representations of death and rebirth. Most of these late stories are greatly illuminated by an understanding of Jungian thought. The Jungian system, like the others London uses in his works, provides a key not only to the works themselves, but also to the understanding of the author's attempt to find his own personal salvation.*

In his intelligent characterization of naturalism, Donald Pizer identifies a central thematic tension in naturalistic fiction between "the naturalist's desire to represent in fiction the new, discomforting truth which he has found in the ideas and life of his late nineteenth-century world, and also his desire to find some meaning in experience which reasserts the validity of the human enterprise."[1] For Jack London, certainly, this was the dynamic tension behind his intellectual life and fiction. In London's language, there was a struggle between "white logic" (the "antithesis of life") and "the sane and normal order of truth... that life must believe in order to live."[2]

[1] *Realism and Naturalism in Nineteenth-Century American Literature* (Carbondale, Ill., 1966), p. 13.
[2] *John Barleycorn* (New York, 1913), p. 308.

Like Martin Eden, his autobiographical hero, his literary mission was to avoid reductive portrayals of man as either a "clod" or a "god" while admitting both human limitations and heaven-sent possibilities.[3] His protagonists would challenge a stultifying environment and discover "things wonderful."[4]

Since, for London, science had dislodged idealistic concepts of man, his temperament insisted that affirmations of the human condition, too, have a scientifically justifiable rationale. Early in his career, for example, he had used his enthusiastic reading of Haeckel, Darwin, and Spencer to evoke "the stinging things of the spirit" in his famous Alaskan fiction. A few years later he used "scientific" Marxism to dramatize the energy of "the people" in his socialist stories. It is not generally recognized, however, that in the last year of his life Jack London wrote a group of short stories whose scientific authority derived from his reading of Carl Jung's *Psychology of the Unconscious* in Beatrice M. Hinkle's 1916 edition.[5] In 1916 he was once again captivated by a theoretician who proffered him a scientifically defensible rationale for subscribing to humanly sustaining values as he flirted dangerously with nihilism. These last stories are a record of the recurrent philosophical-psychological pattern in his life and fiction—a movement from an excited sense that revelation is at hand to a bitter and enervating disillusionment.

How indebted to *Psychology of the Unconscious* he was is clearly established in the last Alaskan story London wrote—"Like Argus of the Ancient Times."[6] According to Jung, a wandering hero, representing "ever-restless desire," undertakes a perilous "night journey" into a mysterious land, representing a subconscious secret, in search of the "treasure difficult to attain" (*P*, pp. 185-233). Late in the journey the sun-hero wanderer faces death, and this confrontation is, ironically, "the highest summit of life" (*P*, p. 320).[7] Finally, the hero returns to water (the womb) and/or emerges in the east reborn. Analogously in "Argus," Tarwater, the seventy-year-old protagonist who is called "Old Hero" and "Father Christmas," is driven by gold "fever" to search for treasure and becomes lost in a heavy Arctic

[3] *Martin Eden,* Reinhart edition (New York, 1956), p. 212.

[4] *Barleycorn,* p. 113.

[5] *Psychology of the Unconscious: A Study of the Transformation and Symbolisms of the Libido—A Contribution of the Evolution of Thought* (New York). Hereafter cited in the text as *P*. Charmian London mentions that Jack owned this volume and underlined various passages in it. (*The Book of Jack London,* New York, 1921), II, 353.

[6] *The Red One* (New York, 1918). Hereafter cited in the text as *R*.

[7] This Jungian phrase, as well as concept, was anticipated in London's fiction years before as a basic irony in many of his stories: the act of killing creates an ecstasy which "marks the summit of life," he wrote in *The Call of the Wild,* Bantam edition (New York, 1963), p. 49.

snowfall during the long night of winter (*R*, pp. 135, 107). As Tarwater comes close to death and drifts between consciousness and unconsciousness, London describes the state of his character's awareness in Jungian terminology:

> more and more time he spent in his torpor, unaware of what was day-dream and what was sleep-dream in the content of his unconsciousness....
>
> Old Tarwater... recovered, within himself, the infantile mind of the child-man of the early world... and went to myth-making, and sunheroizing, himself hero-maker and the hero in quest of the immemorable treasure difficult of attainment....
>
> Either must he attain the treasure—for so ran the inexorable logic of the shadow-land of the unconscious—or else sink into the all-devouring sea, the blackness eater of the light that swallowed to extinction the sun each morning in the east, and that had become to man man's first symbol of immortality through rebirth.... (*R*, pp. 129-130)

Finally, Tarwater "turned his back on the perilous west and limped into the sunarising, rebirthing east" where he discovers gold (*R*, p. 133).

Not just this passage, of course, but almost the entire story is cast in Jungian concepts. The most pervasive of these, and perhaps the most personally significant to London, is Jung's concept of the libido. It allowed London, once again attempting serious fiction after four years of turning out potboilers, to resurrect his analogous concepts of "true adventure" and "imagination"—those prerequisite capacities for embracing the hardships in nature and wresting spiritual regeneration from a nightmarish encounter with the Arctic wasteland.[8]

In his copy of *Psychology of the Unconscious,* London had underscored this definition of "libido" by Dr. Hinkle: "He, Jung, saw in the term libido a concept of unknown nature, comparable with Bergson's élan vital, a hypothetical energy of life,... [a] cosmic energy or urge manifested in the human being [and like] the energy of physics" (*P*, xxvi).[9] The restless wanderer, Tarwater, is driven by his often mentioned "fever" which is equivalent to the "unquenchable longing" of libido energy working within the sun-hero, making him continue his perilous journey (*P*, pp. 230-231). His eastward movement and discovery of gold (which has the color of sun and fire and is therefore associated with libido) indicate the measure of Tarwater's success

[8]"True adventure" as opposed to false is distinguished frequently by London in his Alaskan fiction: see, for example, "In a Far Country," *The Son of the Wolf* (New York, 1900), p. 72. For a discussion of London's concept of "imagination," see Earle Labor, "Jack London's Symbolic Wilderness: Four Versions," *Nineteenth-Century Fiction,* XVII (Sept., 1962), 151-152.

[9]Charmian London, p. 358.

in releasing his libido energy and, simultaneously, revitalizing it (*P*, p. III). And "if one honors God, the sun or the fire," Jung writes, "then one honors one's own vital force, the libido" (*P*, p. 96). If one reverses this statement, the quality of London's affirmation is captured: if one honors one's vital force by participating in true adventure, he honors life. London had found in Jung's libido concept a new rationale for suggesting, as he had suspected early in his career, that man has an internal energy equivalent to the hostile natural forces crushing in upon him.

London must have sensed that the Alaskan materials had been fully exploited and that, despite the new Jungian language, he did little more in "Argus" than he had done earlier and more artistically years before. The other five Jungian stories, impressive for their dramatic unity, simplicity, and thematic kinship with London's best fictions and all collected in *On the Makaloa Mat,* use materials from his adopted second home of Hawaii.[10]

Taking their cue from Charmian London's biography of her husband, several critics have recognized the Jungian basis for "When Alice Told Her Soul." Ironically, it is the only one of these last stories which can be fully understood without knowing Jungian doctrine or symbolism; but the theme of this comic story is derived from a passage in *Psychology of the Unconscious* in which Jung claims that the libido can be released from disturbing subconscious secrets and can find creative outlets if the troubled person confesses his secrets (*P*, p. 233).[11] Alice Akana, the troubled person, runs an exclusive "hula house" where, over the years, she has learned the indiscretions of Honolulu's social elite. Abel Ah Yo, a Bill Sunday style of evangelist, awakens a desire for redemption in her but tells her that she must make a public confession if she is to be redeemed. At this point, the narrator intrudes in order to establish his awareness of the new science of psychology: "Scientifically, though he did not know it and though he continually jeered at science, Abel Ah Yo was right.... The result of such a baring would be unity, tranquility, happiness, cleansing, redemption and immortal life" (*M*, p. 84). Although Alice says, "This rebirth is difficult," "The penitent Phyrne" unburdens her soul of Honolulu's social secrets and sets the rollicking good humor into motion (*M*, p. 85).

The only other comic story in the volume, "The Tears of Ah Kim," seems to be an eccentric thematically obscure piece of slapstick. Actually it is almost a programmatic presentation of specific symbols and themes discussed in *Psychology of the Unconscious.* Mrs. Tai

[10]New York, 1919. Hereafter cited in the text as *M*.

[11]Charmian London, p. 353.

Fu has always beaten Ah Kim, her fifty-year-old son, with a bamboo stick, the current reason for the punishment being her disapproval of Li Faa, Ah Kim's fiancée. Although he has always accepted, even relished the beatings, one day the customary lashing causes him to cry for the first time. Shortly afterward, the mother dies and Ah Kim marries Li Faa. The central question, one critic asked recently, is why Ah Kim does not "weep under the beating of his mother's bamboo stick until a certain day."[12]

One suspects that some aspect of the oedipal complex is the intellectual rationale behind the unusual action. In fact, London has dramatized a corollary to the oedipal attachment theory—Jung's concept of "the sacrifice" which is the substance of the last chapter of *Psychology of the Unconscious.* Ah Kim must undergo the pain which derives both from the guilt that springs from his incestuous impulses and his desire to be punished for his rebellious instincts. The bamboo stick, "predominantly a mother symbol," signifies that Mrs. Tai Fu's instrument of authority and punishment is her motherhood, and its phallic connotations reinforce Ah Kim's incestuous guilt (*P*, p. 264). Ah Kim's "submissive and yielding attitude . . . over-compensates for the rebellion and reaction within" (*P,* xxxiv).

To overcome guilt and achieve maturity, Jung writes in his chapter "The Sacrifice," a person must find a "sexual object" to "replace the forbidden mother" (p. 459). This, of course explains the increasing importance of Li Faa in the story as Ah Kim goes through the painful process of sacrificing his infantile wishes in order to transfer his libido energy to another object. In addition, Jung writes, freedom from the mother is symbolized in myths by an allusion to death which is followed by the new, mature relationship which evokes a sense of "eternal germination and renewal" and floral imagery (*P*, pp. 436, 467). It is by Jungian design, then, that at the end of "The Tears of Ah Kim" the mother loses her strength and dies, allowing Ah Kim to marry Li Faa. On his wedding night, Ah Kim explains to his bride why he cried under his mother's last beating: "She no longer had strength enough to hurt me' " (*M*, p. 184). His mother had lost her oedipal power. The bride, in a comic allusion to Jung's "eternal germination and renewal" phrase, is described as shaped like a "watermelon seed"; and, completing the cluster of Jungian symbolism for a mature relationship, Ah Kim calls her "my Flower of Serenity, my Perfect Rest" (*M*, p. 184).

Although Jack London had written comedy often before, "When Alice Told Her Soul" and "The Tears of Ah Kim" are unlike the

[12]A. Grove Day, "Introduction," *Stories of Hawaii* (New York, 1965), p. 17.

stories for which he is best remembered, particularly the Alaskan tales. In many of those stories the protagonists had gone on the "long trail" into the threatening "unknown" which "lays a man naked to the very roots of his soul."[13] They exhibited a "pervasive oneiric quality" as figures passed archetypally into the "other world."[14] It is the remaining three Jungian stories in *On the Makaloa Mat*—"The Water Baby," "Shin Bones," and "The Bones of Kahelili"— which testify to the influence of Jungian thought in restoring to London's last fiction these more important characteristics. Imbued with mythic overtones, they examine the threatening contents of the unconscious and, it is broadly hinted, London's own subconscious in particular. Both London's last biographer, Richard O'Connor, and his earliest, Charmian London, have recognized that his interest in Jung was rooted in his personal concerns. The quality of his fascination with psychology, writes O'Connor, was that of "a man sliding down the face of a cliff and grabbing at rocks and bushes to stay his fall."[15] His wife testified that he was ready "to face his naked soul... but that was not new with him. It was the old tragedy that began with his earliest probings."[16] Just as in his youth he had turned with enthusiasm toward Darwin, Spencer, and Marx only to be confronted eventually with disillusionment, his initial enthusiasm for Jung turned to a quiet despair.

"The Water Baby," the last story he wrote, is charged with a simple, lyrical beauty of the kind that had not infused his stories since the Northland tales. And like those first stories, his major theme is the conflict of modern skepticism, born of rationality, with a primitive affirmation whose source is nonrational. Desiring the last, London always was drawn inevitably toward the first. In this story, a modern skeptic named John Lakana (London's own Hawaiian name), fishing with Kohokumu, an aged Hawaiian, lends "a weary ear" to the old man's chants of Hawaiian myths and dieties, particularly of Maui, who had slowed the sun, rearranged the heavenly bodies, fished the land up from under the sea and whom Jung associates with oedipal rebirth mythology (*P*, p. 534). Lakana discusses with Kohokumu Christian and Polynesian mythologies, their basis in scientific theories of evolution, the nature of dreams, and, ultimately, the meaning of life and death.

[13]*The Son of the Wolf,* p. 72. This pattern is so common that it occurs in four stories in London's first volume of short stories alone: "White Silence," "Wisdom of the Trail," "In a Far Country," and "An Odyssey of the North."

[14]Earle Gene Labor, "Jack London's Literary Artistry: His Symbolism in Relation to His Themes" (doctoral dissertation, University of Wisconsin, 1961), p. 66.

[15]*Jack London: A Biography* (Boston, 1964), p. 391.

[16]Charmian London, pp. 355-356.

In these discussions, London explicitly links Kohokumu with the most common natural archetype which Jung identifies with the oedipal myths—that of the sun (the hero and libido energy) setting (dying) in the sea (the womb) and rising in the morning (being reborn). The "secret" of his birth, the old man says, is that "the sea is my mother" (*M*, p. 150). Each time he dives into the sea, he is strengthened, he claims; and in response to this, Lakana thinks, "Shades of Antaeus!" alluding to Jung's commentary upon the story of Antaeus, who could preserve his strength "only through contact with mother earth" (*M*, p. 150; *P*, p. 201). The process of returning to the earth for sustenance symbolizes periodic acts of introversion (*P*, p. 201). Finally, says the old man, he will return to the sea to be reborn:

> when I am really old, I shall be reported as drowned in the sea.... This will be an idle thought of men. In truth, I shall have returned into the arms of my mother, there to rest under the heart of her breast until the second birth of me, when I shall emerge into the sun a flashing youth of splendor like Maui himself when he was golden young. (*M*, p. 150)

During a lull in the fishing, Lakana requests a folk story and Kohokumu obliges him with "The Water Baby," a tale about a young Hawaiian boy who outwits forty sharks in order to catch lobsters for the king and which Charmian London has correctly identified as a "symbolic representation of the Rebirth, the return to the Mother."[17] As he had in "The Tears of Ah Kim," London uses symbols identified by *Psychology of the Unconscious* as connected with libido renewal and growth into emotional maturity. The Water Baby (libido energy, since he speaks the fish language and "the fish is a libido symbol") conquers the sharks (subconscious anxieties, an "incest barrier" which denotes "treasurer guardian" and connotes death) and captures the lobster delicacies (the "treasure difficult of attainment") and thus stays the wrath of the King (avoids destruction and reaffirms life).[18] John Lakana is attentive to the tale, but remains skeptical. The implied tension between civilized skepticism and a natural affirmation of life remains unresolved.

"Shin Bones" also dramatizes the tensions between twentieth-century skepticism and primitive, romantic optimism by invoking Jungian concepts. This time, however, the conflict is within a single character, the modern Hawaiian protagonist, Prince Akuli, who as the last male descendant of the royal family of "Lakanii" (obviously a variant of London's Hawaiian name) is the London surrogate.

[17]Charmian London, p. 354.

[18]*P*, pp. 223, 403, 292.

In "the culminating period of my adolescence" (*M*, p. 142) or, in Jungian terminology, in the final "budding" stage of libido development (*P*, xxix), Akuli was torn between the competing demands of his father, a cynical businessman in whom there was "no sacredness" (*M*, p. 133), and his mother, who had reverted to superstitious ancient Hawaiian beliefs by worshiping at the shrine of ancestral bones. The boy himself "could be a skeptic out in the open in the sunshine... but... was afraid of the dark" (*M*, p. 121).

Prince Akuli tells a confidant that he was once persuaded by his mother to undertake a dangerous trip to the secret Lakanii burial cave. London knew from his reading of *Psychology of the Unconscious* that any mystery or secret place indicates "a subjectively important secret" which "cuts one off from intercourse with the rest of mankind" and that caves symbolize both the womb and the unconscious (*P*, pp. 233, 375). The Lakanii burial cave, then, is London's own unconscious which he must explore if he is to overcome anxiety and alienation. Akuli's guide is "old Ahuna," who, as an "ancient" like Kohokumu in "The Water Baby," is associated by Jung with revitalizing powers of tapping the unconscious (*P*, pp. 207-208). At first the Prince was reluctant to undertake this particular exploration because, like Jack London facing the exploration of his unconscious it is implied, there were more exciting things to discover—"there were North Poles" (*M*, p. 119). He goes nevertheless.

No modern reader can misunderstand the detailed anatomical symbolism of London's depiction of this "night journey" to the secret cave since it is common to both Freud and Jung. Prince Akuli has entered the womb, has descended into his own unconscious where he can examine the "great disturbance" which "cuts one off from intercourse with the rest of mankind." Still in keeping with archetypal symbolism, the Prince has an "illumination" in the cave and learns "the great lesson" which he associates with two bones, from a Hawaiian Lancelot and Guinevere, that he takes back (*M*, pp. 137-138). His "imagination" is "fired" by the romance of the Arthurian legend of manly strength, adventure, and passion in which he had once believed but "sobered" and replaced by "things I dare not name" that are associated with his newfound awareness of human mortality—the traditional direction of London's own emotional patterns (*M*, pp. 138, 141). Like a friend from his youth, "on the edge of the grave" Akuli could "sneer at superstition" of any kind, ancient and modern, his mother's superstitious romanticism and his father's callous materialism (*M*, p. 123).

It would seem, then, that London's trip into his own unconscious gave little comfort to the wealthy man who had enjoyed dramatizing himself as a masculine adventurer and heroic lover and who was suffering from physical deterioration and emotional turmoil during the last days of his life. That London's use of Jungian conceptions had turned from a celebration of life's vitality to a final pessimistic preoccupation with death evidenced in this story is reinforced by the last Jungian Hawaiian story—"The Bones of Kahelili."

As do "The Water Baby" and "Shin Bones," the stories which reveal the darker side of London's imagination, "The Bones of Kahelili" uses the Jungian concept of an "ancient" revealing a "secret" about the mystery of death to a London surrogate. In this story Hardman Pool, like Jack London at his Glen Ellen ranch, is a wealthy, benevolent patriarch of a Hawaiian plantation who has become jaded through the effects of drink and age. To entertain himself, Pool asks an old retainer, Kumuhana, to reveal the secret of where Chief Kahelili is buried. In response, the old man tells him a tale. When he was a young man about to risk mortal combat for his love, Kumuhana was selected to accompany the burial canoe of Kahelili as a human sacrifice. When the glass-covered coffin was thrown overboard, it would not sink, showing the grotesque face of the corpse, until a horrified priest broke the glass. The ritual disturbed, Kumuhana escaped his fate and became the only living person who knows the story.

Without an understanding of London's Jungian interest in libido theory and its revelation in myths, this story is puzzling. London, I believe, suggests a hierarchy of "natural obligations" which culminates in death and implies the impossibility of spiritual renewal. "The desire for woman must be greater than the desire for life," Pool extrapolates from the old man's story, since Kumuhana would risk death to win a bride; and obedience to authority is stronger than both since he abandons love to obey the royal command to become a sacrifice (*M*, pp. 59-61). What remains implicit is that death is a final obligation stronger than life, love, or obedience. Reflecting upon the story, Hardman Pool is most impressed by the mythic significance of one of the death chants used in the funeral ritual:

> But death is nothing new.
> Death is and has been ever since old Maui died.
> Then Pata-tai laughed loud
> And woke the goblin god,
> Who severed him in two, and shut him in,
> So dusk of eve came on. (*M*, p. 72)

The riddle of death and rebirth is solved by suggesting the finality of death, the theme implicit in "Shin Bones." Maui the sun god of rebirth is dead; or, in other terms, the libido or will to live is dead. The destructive "goblin god" rules, bringing "the dusk of eve," a phrase which obsesses Pool and in which he finds "an intense satisfaction" (*M*, p. 76).

It is appropriate that London uses the grotesque at the end of Kumuhana's tale since grotesquery had been synonymous with the overwhelming, malign powers that crushed out life in the Alaskan stories. The protagonists in those stories, like London's autobiographical Hardman Pool, were left without the psychic energy necessary for actively engaging in a contest with death.

Throughout his career, it had been Jack London's scientific reading and personal adventures which accounted for the themes and materials of his fiction: at first it was Darwin linked with the Klondike and at last Jung with Hawaii. And first and last, London had been preoccupied with a search for salvation amidst hints of certain damnation. As a self-styled "hopeless materialist," a "monist" in Haeckel's sense of the word, he was much given to a quest for revelation; the basis for that revelation had to be "scientific," of course, explaining his enthusiastic acceptance of reductive systems whether they came from Herbert Spencer or Carl Jung.[19] London even suggested in the person of his recurring Alaskan hero, the Malemute Kid, as he did again in old Tarwater, that the scientifically warranted revelation is available to those who exercise "imagination" or release "libido" energy and who take the prerequisite risks.[20] For Jack London, Jung's *Psychology of the Unconscious* was the last in a series of romantic calls to completion, to self-identifying and self-sustaining values that would assure man of his nobility.

Despite the celebration of nobility, like that in "Argus," and despite the playful entertainment of positive values like the belief in a dynamic life force which London portrayed in comedies like "When Alice Told Her Soul" and "The Tears of Ah Kim," the romantic call always before had led, and did again in 1916, to reminders of impotence and mortality and, consequently, to disillusionment. London portrayed man in a contest to discover his soul amidst trials of the flesh: his fiction had characteristically revealed a tension between equivalents of old Kohokumu's spiritual vitality and John Lakana's physical-psychological deterioration in "The Water Baby," between Prince Akuli's romantic imagination and his modern skepticism in "Shin Bones," and between Kumuhana's knowledge of life and Hardman Pool's jaded awareness of death in "The Bones of Kahelili." From the beginning of his career, the battle between spirit and flesh had been central to London's life, his literary esthetic,

[19] *Letters from Jack London*, ed. King Hendricks and Irving Shepard (New York, 1965), p. 425.

[20] The Malemute Kid is the masculine ideal and the moral norm in six of the stories in *The Son of the Wolf* including the famous "White Silence" and "An Odyssey of the North."

and his fictions. Certain that the godlike in man would triumph, he pitted man's subjective powers against the positivistic facts of life, whether those facts were symbolically present in the Alaskan landscape or in a protagonist's aging body.

But while the mature Alaskan stories dramatized the tragedy of youthful, energetic protagonists testing their vitality against the brutal forces of nature only to be drawn catastrophically toward the demonic, the irrational and death-dealing, these last few stories reveal a shift in mood. They dramatize the pathos of aging and disillusioned, even cynical, men awaiting death. While violence and death, the triumph of the demonic, had somehow surprised the earlier protagonists, these last—Jack Lakana, Prince Akuli, and Hardman Pool—are without the capacity for amazement. Carl Jung's system as Jack London found it in *Psychology of the Unconscious,* like the other systems he had found before, had failed on the eve of his suicide to give him a sure faith. Hardman Pool voices a sentiment which might be taken as the cast of London'a own last thoughts: "We are wise, but the wisdom is bitter" (*M*, p. 70).

Androgyny in the Novels of Jack London

CLARICE STASZ

London's concern with physical strength and with what many consider a "macho" world makes his treatment of women a subject of much interest to London readers. Professor Stasz offers here a discussion of a number of London novels. These writings illustrate clearly London's attempts to break down some of the traditional stereotypes and expectations concerning sex-role behavior. The virtues that the male and female characters in these novels exhibit are virtues determined by qualities often traditionally assigned to the opposite sex. Implied in London's portrayal of sex roles is a criticism of the traditional narrow American definition of male and female roles in our society. Although London never completely abandoned some traditional views of male superiority, he came closer than his contemporaries to breaking down the stereotypes of sex roles.

Around the turn of the century, new possibilities were beginning to open up for American women.[1] A type popularly referred to as the "New Woman" began to appear: well-educated, athletic, unchaperoned. Most middle-class women seemed to prefer marriage and domesticity, but the New Women were proud of single independence. The women in Jack London's life illustrate both role choices. Both Mabel Applegarth, his fiancée, and Bess Maddern, his first wife, followed the conventional pattern, while his friend Anna Strunsky, his sister, Eliza Shepard, and most distinctly his second wife Charmian Kittredge resembled the New Woman in some respects.

[1]See Peter Gabriel Filene, *Him/Her/Self* (New York: Harcourt Brace, Jovanovich, 1974); Robert W. Smuts, *Women and Work in America* (New York: Columbia University Press, 1959); Theodore P. Green, *America's Heroes* (New York: Oxford University Press, 1970).

Men at the time also faced problems concerning their identity. Work moved from outdoors to the bureaucracy, a setting which gave men little opportunity to display the 'manly' virtues of self-reliance, courage, or resoluteness. Few could achieve material wealth, the measure of success. Men were raised to think of themselves as beasts driven by sexual appetite, yet also were encouraged to be sexually pure. Media critics attacked men for the social ills of the new urban-industrial society and for neglecting their homes. Obviously, the pressures on individual males were considerable, and somewhat contradictory.

London's life again illustrates these ambivalences. He drank to be a man, a stout fellow, while secretly he disliked alcohol. He married and became a father, but was not responsible to the family in the way society demanded. Material wealth did not bring satisfaction, because he still felt the need to express superior self-reliance and courage in many endeavors. Nothing that he did seemed sufficient to make him a 'man.' His male friends, George Sterling for example, also exhibited signs of personal strain in trying to meet the unclear expectations concerning masculinity.

London's writings reflect, among other things, an attempt to resolve some of the cultural contradictions and ambiguities concerning gender behavior. Most notably, his novels display the development of a radical, visionary conception of masculinity and femininity. In this paper I shall examine some of London's novels chronologically so that developmental changes in his thought can be identified.

The societal ambivalences concerning sex roles appear in London's first novel, *A Daughter of the Snows.*[2] Frona Welse, the heroine, is a dynamic woman of a type rare in American fiction. In the first chapter she proudly brags how she can swing clubs, box, fence, swim, do high dives, and walk on her hands. Having returned to Alaska from college, she displays her knowledge of the frontier on the trek inward to Dawson, during which men drop injured and dead around her. Once ensconced in her father's home, she becomes the Lady, entertaining guests, playing piano, and performing as Nora in *The Doll's House.* Yet she wears short (ankle-length) skirts and even befriends a town prostitute. Though "independent in some ways" Frona accepts a future of domestic life. As the book develops, she puts aside her athletic antics and increasingly represents woman as a moral force. Critics call her 'unrealistic' as a character because of her physical prowess. But if she is unrealistic it is because it is more likely that a woman of her type would have become a 'bachelor woman' and ruled the area as her father did. To call her prowess

[2]Jack London, *A Daughter of the Snows* (New York: Grosset and Dunlap, 1902).

'unrealistic' is to overlook the fact that other women of the day did match Frona's accomplishments.

The male characters in this novel are more notable. Frona's father, Jacob Welse, is the patriarch of the colony, a man who succeeded through what was then called 'character'—the application of his brains in a tough, competitive, yet honest way. He also succeeded at home, as is indicated by his loving relationship with his daughter. Welse is the other moral force in the book.

The competition of the admirers for Frona is implicitly a debate concerning masculinity. Vance Corliss is an effete Yale man who hesitantly, though successfully, proves that he has the mettle for frontier life. He has difficulty accepting Frona because she is not ignorant about sex and is at ease with her sexual feelings. She also traps Vance with her logical repartées. When he is angry over her visiting with the prostitute Lucile, Frona notes that he can hardly be spotless.

> "But I am—"
> "A man of course. Very good. Because you are a man, you may court contamination. Because I am a woman, I may not. Contamination contaminates, does it not? Then you, what do you here with me?" (pp. 108-9)

So much for the double standard.

Gregory St. Vincent is more blatantly 'masculine'—making claims (later disproven) to brave adventures and being the most accomplished gentleman in town. Yet there are hints throughout the novel that he is a coward. Through a series of melodramatic and unbelievable incidents, Gregory's lack of character is uncovered and he loses Frona. He fails to exhibit courage, and more importantly, violates the frontier "faith of food and blanket." Thus appearances of manliness do not make a man, for action and their character are what matter. The only curious feature of the male characters' behaviors is their attraction to a New Woman such as Frona.

Written close upon a time of deep personal troubles and self-analysis, *The Sea-Wolf* questions rigidity in sex roles.[3] On a psychological level, the interplay of Wolf Larsen and Humphrey Van Weyden reminds one of Jung's concept of animus and anima, the male and female parts of the self. Wolf is the super*man*: arrogant, domineering, crafty, aloof, alone. Van Weyden, like Vance Corliss, begins the book as a fearful, aesthetic intellectual with social openness. Van Weyden develops the more 'masculine' qualities during his stay on the *Ghost*, and in doing so develops to full self-maturity. As if

[3]Jack London, *The Sea-Wolf* (New York: Macmillan, 1904).

to emphasize the importance of being both masculine and feminine, Van Weyden muses on how he had been raised among women, and how "It has dawned on me that I never placed a proper valuation upon womankind." (p. 128) As for the *Ghost* with its all-male world:

> Coarseness and savagery are the inevitable results.... There is no balance in their lives. Their masculinity, which in itself is of the brute, has been overdeveloped. (p. 129)

With this stated philosophy, relationship with a woman would be a likely path to final maturity for Van Weyden, and so Maude Brewster appears.

Maude is the most ethereal and idealized of all London's female characters, but she demonstrates elements of his personal ideal, the mate-woman.[4] Maude behaves with courage and vigor, although her dress and sexuality reflect Victorian proprieties. She completes Van Weyden's growth because he must become responsible for someone else. Social concern and co-operation are to temper individualism. In dramatizing this synthesis, London was right in line with his times. As Filene[5] describes the period:

> An irony [in male attitudes] had emerged. While decrying women who become 'masculinized' by entering the realm outside kitchen and parlor, men were plagiarizing the women's social values. In so doing, they acknowledge not only a modified definition of their own role, but also a larger female sphere; the public realm belonged, more than before, to both sexes. The "New Woman" was called in to redress the imbalances of the old masculine world. (p. 84)

The Iron Heel[6] is unique in that the narrator is a woman, Avis Everhard, who reports of her political activities with her husband Ernest. As in London's real life, the marriage is one of a working-class man with a middle-class woman. Avis succumbs to Ernest because he combines strength in body and intellect with "a delicate and sensitive spirit" and is a tender lover. In London's view he is a total "man." Marriage does not domesticate Avis. She develops her secretarial skills to work with Ernest. Like so many London characters she behaves fearlessly during times of physical danger. The marriage through its moral force bonds the comradeship, though it little resembles marriages of the day, which were not so equalitarian.

[4]Soon after completing *The Sea-Wolf* London wrote his ideas concerning the mate-woman in a love letter to Charmian. Such a woman was the equivalent of the man-comrade, one who combined courage, assertiveness, and imagination (in this culture 'masculine' qualities) with tenderness, sensitivity, and forgiveness ('feminine' qualities). For the full text see Charmian London, *The Book of Jack London* (New York: Century, 1921),Volume 2, pp. 81-83.

[5]Filene, *Him/Her/Self*, p. 84.

[6]Jack London, *The Iron Heel* (New York: Macmillan, 1908).

Martin Eden[7] traces the labored steps toward Martin's writing success, his courtship with Ruth, his fiancée, and his suicide. The book is a piercing view of a young working-class man of the times who dares to succeed.[8] Once successful, he learns that for the middle class love seems a commodity. The book must have shocked many readers' sensibilities. How could Martin choose suicide over marriage to Ruth, the ideal Victorian lady? London hints at what is to come and why, when he has Martin's friend Brissenden say:

> "Pick out some great, wanton flame of a woman, who laughs at life, jeers at death, and loves one while she may. There are other such women . . . prattling out little moralities that have been prattled into them, and afraid to live life. They will love you, Martin, but they will love their little moralities more" (p. 245).

What clearer rejection of the Lady? And in this plot, too, there is a recognition that women are not innately redeemers of *man*kind. Society, particularly through social class, structures men and women alike to be insensitive and inhumane. This knowledge is a sophisticated sociological insight, and a key to Martin's death. He lacked that woman who laughs at life; he could no longer bear the bleakness of working-class culture; he could not accept the hypocrisy and venality of the middle class. Readers viewed his choice as immoral and unmanly: "In his bitterness he weakly throws away all that his strength has won"[9] said one reviewer.

In *Burning Daylight*[10] London intertwines several of the themes developed in his earlier novels. Elam Harnish is the male Klondike counterpart of Frona Welse. His drive for mastery continues unabated following a series of accomplishments. He succeeds in two male worlds: the male frontier, where he is called Daylight, and the Robber Baron arena of finance. As with the men on the *Ghost,* he becomes hardened, self-indulgent, suspicious, and immoral. His salvation occurs partly in the form of his secretary Dede Mason, a New Woman who lives in Berkeley, dates college men, and keeps a horse. In time a romance develops. When Daylight proposes, Dede is confused. She does not approve of his acquisitiveness and his behavior toward others. Yet she considers how well she can care for herself without the usual "feminine fears and timidities." Marriage

[7]Jack London, *Martin Eden* (New York: Macmillan, 1909).

[8]Though a minor character, Martin's sister illustrates London's understanding of how poverty combines with the patriarchal family structure to virtually enslave the working-class female. Similarly, his descriptions of working-class jobs, notably Martin's work in a laundry, are harrowingly realistic and help explain why men in such jobs drink and mistreat their wives.

[9]Anonymous plot summary, *Book Review Digest,* 1909.

[10]Jack London, *Burning Daylight* (New York: Macmillan, 1910).

would be a 'little thing' to a woman such as she, whose life was satisfying, but humdrum. Dede finally tells Daylight that she cannot marry him because his money possesses him. Eventually he renounces his wealth and delights in the forces of Dede's love and the Sonoma wilderness.

It is most appropriate that Elam is an anagram of Male because this novel presents various turn-of-the-century attitudes toward masculinity. The Klondike episodes are nostalgic for the male 1910 reader, with their examples of men using their brains and courage to master the wilderness. Women have little place there. (Love to Daylight was like "smallpox," "delirium tremens," and "stark lunacy.") Once in civilization, Daylight encounters the business image of masculinity where money and competitive wiles measure success. In rejecting this world Daylight agrees with those social critics of the time who deplored male preoccupation with materialism and its consequent social ills. By implication, the conclusion undermines the comfortable notions of femininity and masculinity held by conventional society. Proof that his radical message was received is found in the acerbic New York *Times* review:

> A love story must at least have a man and a woman in it. And this has neither. It was in short, twaddle with the T sharp.[11]

Perhaps because of its embarrassing racist ideology, *Adventure*[12] has been ignored by recent critics. It is relevant here nonetheless, if only because the hero, David Sheldon, is so well-drawn a caricature of what would be called today a "male chauvinist." An inhumane overseer of cannibal workers on a plantation in the Solomon Islands, he is totally secure with his exploitative beliefs. (He also lives in terror for his life.) As the London devotee might predict, a pistol-packing woman arrives to show him the error of his ways. Joan Lackland manages to prove herself right and Sheldon wrong in the series of adventures that follow. For much of the book he handles her in his mind as many men do when faced with such a skillful female—he desexualizes her and calls her a "boy." He keeps telling himself she will fail, when in fact she continues to succeed.

Joan is a benevolent matriarch toward her workers. She often reminds Sheldon that her interest is only in managing a plantation, not in marriage. When a second eligible white man arrives on the scene her attitude changes. Sheldon demonstrates his possessiveness by challenging the suitor to a duel. Totally out of character, Joan gives in to the argument that she must marry Sheldon to preserve

[11]New York *Times*, November 5, 1910.

[12]Jack London, *Adventure* (New York: Macmillan, 1911).

their reputation among the islands so that other men do not abuse her. Thus social purity is saved, and a man gains maturity through the guidance of a woman.

Throughout much American or English fiction and drama the working-class woman is either a prostitute or a drudge. Saxon Brown of *The Valley of the Moon*[13] is a refreshing contrast. We are given the realities of life for such women: the tedium and torture of the workshops; the tense family life; the hurried gaity at rare social events. We watch Saxon's outlook mature from its romantic and domestic thoughts to political realism. She and her husband, Billy Roberts, begin marriage by mimicking what they can of the middle-class mode. They buy a houseful of furniture on time and Saxon stays home doing domestic work, secretly sewing to make extra money. When Billy's union activities lead him to ignore her, to drink, and eventually to go to jail, Saxon meets tests of her character. She enters a period of emotional turmoil, but emerges with a new vision for Billy and herself, one that will lead to a better life.

Billy's personality is better developed in the first section of the book, where he is embroiled in wooing Saxon and in fighting for the union. Once the striving for a new home begins, he, like Saxon, behaves more mechanically. London's political disenchantment comes through when Billy gives up the working-class struggle to seek a new life. He is no Ernest Everhard. Even the revolution is no longer a place for a man to mature. So he mimics Daylight, another self-chosen outcast, and settles for ranch life in Sonoma. Perhaps this is why the New York *Times* gave London a positive review, saying the book was "a man's size book, containing a man's size idea."[14]

The last book of note here, *Little Lady of the Big House,*[15] is possibly the most misunderstood. The plot, a weak and tedious one, concerns a triangle: Dick Forrest, a rancher, Paula Forrest, his frenetically talented wife, and Evan Graham, an adventurer and guest at the ranch. Although Dick plans suicide once he learns of his wife's attachments to Graham, Paula shoots herself instead. Given certain superficial resemblances between Dick and Paula with Jack and Charmian, some critics argue that the book represents an unconscious desire on London's part to see Charmian dead.[16] However, evidence from the time of the writing suggests that London was devoted to Charmian, although the relationship had been through periods of

[13]Jack London, *The Valley of the Moon* (New York: Macmillan, 1913).

[14]New York *Times*, November 9, 1913.

[15]Jack London, *The Little Lady of the Big House,* (New York: Macmillan, 1916).

[16]The best example of such an argument is Kevin Starr, *Californians and the American Dream* (New York: Oxford University Press, 1973).

difficulty.[17] The psychological interpretation ignores other material in the book, as well as the climate in which it was written. London also obscures his intentions with his oblique style. Labor notes that the book exhibits "an undercurrent of irony and... an atmosphere of decadence, which may not have been conscious in intent."[18]

In the first chapter, Dick is in his workroom, a model of efficiency. A woman's boudoir cap belies sexual activity, but this clue may have been placed to throw the reader off. We follow Dick through his daily routines, and always he acts in a decisive, firm, direct, rationalistic style. In a discussion with a foreman, Dick states his attitude toward women:

> "...Our own human females...are intrinsically maternal. There is no biological sanction for all the hurly burly of woman today for suffrage and career." (p. 21)

We then learn that the Forrests are childless. After rough-housing with three young female guests, Forrest notes that he is four minutes late for an appointment. Efficiency rules.

A millionaire's son, Forrest was sent to public schools, where he learned to become a social diplomat. When orphaned, he shocked his guardians by taking to the road, where he learned, he says, that "reality never lied" (p. 58). Continuing his schooling and later adventures, "he never achieved super-excellence at anything...[but] he failed at nothing" (pp. 59-60). At 30 he married Paula Desten, also from a socially 'great' family.

Paula first appears in Dick's office, where he goes into a recurrent chant, "I am Eros. I stamp upon the hills." She notes how he keeps his hand marking his place in a pamphlet and glances at the clock. He misses how her voice is subdued when she leaves.

London builds up a view of the cold-blooded American male, superb at managing objects, animals, and workers, yet out of touch with his feelings and insensitive to the possibility of genuine intimacy. Forrest is a boor. He dominates intellectual exchanges among his guests, entertains dubiously with his Indian chants, and expresses a subtle sadism toward guests and workers. Though he claims to love Paula, he ignores her needs and embarrasses her in public.

Paula is the perfect victim, the trapped princess in the tower. She copes by developing her skills in various areas: animal breeding, horseback riding, swimming, piano. Dick doesn't understand her interest in embroidery because he can buy better work than she can make. Nothing she does is of value to him unless it betters others or earns profit. He calls her his boy, in a parallel to David Sheldon's

[17] I will discuss this evidence in a forthcoming biography of Charmian.

[18] Earle Labor, *Jack London* (New York: Twayne, 1974), p. 143.

desexualization of Joan Lackland. Like so many of London's heroines, Paula is physically fearless, though in this case her athletics seem less an expression of self-assertion than the desperate act of one having little to lose in case of failure.

London gives Paula spiritual qualities that are lost in quick reading. The point of her insomnia is that she learned to live with it, to "win through an undertow" (p. 152). Elsewhere she explains to Graham that she just does things, while Dick must learn everything ahead of time and be in control. Paula says she breeds animals in a "witchlike" and "intuitional" way. Had London stayed with the philosophical differences between Dick and Paula, the novel could have modelled the structure of *The Sea-Wolf,* where conflicts in personality mirror conflicts in philosophy.

Instead, as in *The Sea-Wolf,* the competing love interest interferes in a devastating way. Evan Graham is an enigma, for like an adolescent in first love he spends most of his time mooning over Paula. Paula's attraction to him is curious, for his appeal is not clearly described. Forrest continues to be preoccupied with his work, to ignore Paula's attempts for intimacy, to discount any possibility of affection between Paula and Graham. At several points Paula openly criticizes Forrest's intellectual outpourings, as for example:

> "Words, words, words . . . I don't know what bearing sporting dominants and race-paces have on my life. They show me no right or wrong way for my particular feet" (p. 259).

But these criticisms are not developed sufficiently, so Paula seems like a nagger, when in fact her attacks are cogent and meaningful.

Forrest's behavior reinforces Graham's and Paula's mutual attraction, though unwittingly. Over the years he has encouraged and come to expect guests to be attracted to Paula. Thus, he treats her as property, for she serves as a symbolic extension of his ego. Like many achievement-oriented persons, he does not see how he could be failing her because he is the very model of success.

Paula becomes more confused. She admires Forrest for being a great man; Graham, for being a great lover. She tells Graham that the triangle "must be solved for me" (p. 320). Graham's love makes her husband seem pitiable to her, and she cannot abide that. Yet,

> "Let come what would . . . she would play it out. It was all a madness, but it was life, it was living. She had never lived before, and it was worth it" (p. 325).

Later, in talking with Dick, she seems to accept responsibility for what has occurred:

> "Shaw and the rest must be right. Women are hunting animals. You are both big game . . . I want you. I want Evan" (p. 367).

After discussing a divorce with her husband, she returns to see him. She looks in and discovers, "There he was, with his love-world crashing around him, calmly considering dams" (p. 375). As for Evan, she feels her lust for him could not fulfill her because he lacked Dick's greatness. Death seems to be Paula's only choice if she is to be true to herself. Neither Dick nor Evan alone can complete her, and the society of the time seemingly allows her no other apparent options. She has been treated like a child, then left by both men to solve a situation difficult even for persons with much experience.

Paula's death is the denial of Dick's philosophy of efficiency and rationality. Without her, his one hope for intimacy and fulfillment is lost. For all her talents, Paula has been trapped as a Lady, useless to anyone except a man's ego. She has been held in arrested development through Dick's treatment of her as a boy. She is no freer than those modern women who are allowed no other self-expression than domestic tasks. The tragedy is lost in the farcical treatment of the ending, where Dick chants his Eros song and Paula speaks baby-talk as she dies.

Paula tells Dick she is sorry there were no babies. Previously in the novel we have learned that she is apparently fertile, so why should this couple, so richly productive in individual endeavors, have remained barren? Perhaps it was because the pair were not mature in London's eyes. Paula was in no sense a mate-woman because Dick was in no sense a mature man. He was not:

> ...delicate and tender, brave and game; sensitive as he pleased in the soul of him, and in the body of him unfearing and unwitting of pain.[19]

In a letter to his daughter, London wrote that the ending of *Little Lady* was "the only clean, decent way out."[20] For a woman then to leave a man was considered most immoral because the woman was to be the conservator of society. Even so, the book was shocking to middle-class morality by its hints of dalliance. As a reviewer in the *Atlantic Monthly* wrote:

> *Little Lady* reproduces the facund [sic]—nay glib—erotomania of three persons who fiddle harmonies on the strings of sensualism.[21]

Little Lady shows that the journey from wilderness through civilization to ranch is not the answer to a man's needs. If he retains the traditional male values of American society, he cannot develop

[19]Charmian London, *The Book of Jack London*, p. 82.

[20]King Hendricks and Irving Shepard, *Letters from Jack London* (New York: Odyssey Press, 1965), p. 467.

[21]*Atlantic Monthly*, October, 1916.

fully as a human being. Woman, too, cannot simply by virtue of being female complete man. The middle-class Lady is too retarded in her growth to be of use to others, she is not even of use to herself. The existing system of sex roles thwarts the development of androgyny and inhibits both inner security and a sense of self-worth. *Little Lady* marks the deep pessimism London felt toward the end of his life. London seemed to recognize here that his earlier ethos of single-minded individualism was inadequate and unrealistic. In their sex roles and relationships, where they most need maturity, individuals are fated by cultural prescriptions.

In his real life and in his fiction, Jack London deviated from traditional conceptions of sex roles. He recognized what psychologists and social scientists have documented, that there are many ways in which narrow definitions of masculinity and femininity in American society repress important aspects of personality. His implicit critique can be summarized thus:

1. The mature human personality is androgynous. One should allow all potentialities to be expressed, not just those considered appropriate to one's gender role. The New Woman is the most developed personality in society, and is a model for others, including men.

2. Males who are successful by traditional male standards do not develop important human qualities, such as intimacy or intuition.

3. Females are generally made infant-like by society and kept retarded in development by men's efforts to impose false idealizations of feminity.

4. In spite of societal beliefs, women are capable of performing as well as men at "masculine" tasks, and men can be as sensitive, gentle, and intuitive as women are supposed to be.

5. The class structure is burdening in different ways. It brutalizes working-class men, leading them to drink, and dehumanizes middle-class men, cutting them off from emotions. It enslaves lower-class women by making them drudges or prostitutes, and it imprisons middle-class women in the demands of the Lady role.

6. Women and men can, when both have developed "mature" or androgynous qualities, share in a relationship that is the highest form of love, the mate-comradeship.

7. The cultural values of social purity and marriage are important and should be retained.

With the exception of the last point, these attitudes form what we would call today a nonsexist ideology. However, London's critics and readers tend, understandably, to view him through the dominant sexist ideology. The sexist bias may explain why some readers may misread London's attitudes toward individualism. *The Sea-Wolf* is a notable example, for readers may become so caught by the grandeur of Wolf's masculine superiority and individualism that they fail to see how his death relates to these very qualities. London's most often reprinted book in America remains *The Call of the Wild,* with its all-male dog world and scenes of brutality.

London did not break away fully from sexist values in his life and work. Although he could accept Charmian as a comrade, his treatment of most other women was apparently one of benign neglect. He preferred male friends. He did not question the prevalence of patriarchy in government, the economy, the arts and the family.

Similarly, London's heroines are assertive and talented, but they are never allowed to exist, finally, as leaders or creative persons independent of men. London allows some women to be equal to men, but no matter how talented, they are not to be above men, except as sources of moral inspiration or goodness. Some of London's fictional marriages are models of cooperation and equal respect, but the man still views himself the protector of the woman. His heroines can maintain much high independence within such patriarchy because they are childless and in some cases have domestic servants.

Yet London is notable for drawing images of men who take responsibility for their lives, who are open to criticism and change, even when the criticism comes from a woman. London's successful heroes expect their women to be competent and outspoken, to do their share in serious matters. Such women still puzzle and mystify men, but they are preferred to their classbound sisters. Such men are strong enough to reject the restrictions of the male role, even though rejection may mean suicide. Jack London is no feminist's dream, but he is a male chauvinist's nightmare.

Jack London's Heart of Darkness

SAM BASKETT

London's relationship to other writers and their influence upon him is a subject of much interest to readers. London's relationship with Joseph Conrad has been noted, but it has never been carefully explored. The similarities, while they do not overshadow vast differences between the two writers, focus on man's ironic attempts to find meaning in an ultimately meaningless universe. Professor Baskett notes similarities in two areas. First there are startling parallels (in plot and theme) between London's "In a Far Country" and Conrad's "An Outpost of Progress." Second, similarities in theme are present in London's Martin Eden *and* John Barleycorn *and Conrad's* Heart of Darkness. *In both cases the authors are dealing with a similar problem, the quest for a knowledge of the world, knowledge which leads the characters in all three novels to a confrontation with the evil in man. London has neither the temperence nor the artistic standards of Conrad. However, he touched the same "heart of darkness" which occupied Conrad.*

Although there are certain obvious similarities in the fiction of Jack London and Joseph Conrad—both wrote tales of the sea as well as stories set in exotic lands, and frequently both peopled their fiction with rough characters engaged in violent action—Conrad's different emphasis, surer craftsmanship and more profound insight into the psychological motivations of his characters have made these similarities seem relatively inconsequential. London is often, even within the same book, an exponent of the cult of raw meat and red blood and a political expounder using fiction as a means of advancing the doctrines of socialism. This blatant dichotomy is in obvious contrast to Conrad's characteristically subtle investigations of states of mind. Conrad himself bridled at being regarded "as literarily a sort of Jack London":

> I don't mean to depreciate in the least the talent of the late Jack London, who wrote me in a most friendly way many years ago at the very beginning, I think, of his literary career, and with whom I used to exchange messages through friends afterwards; but the fact remains that temperamentally, mentally, and as a prose writer, I am a different person.[1]

Thus London's biographers and critics have given what seems to be the proper emphasis to the London-Conrad relation when they merely note in a sentence or so that London read the English author and that at one point or another their literary interests coincided extrinsically. Actually, however, it is as misleading to minimize their similarities as to exaggerate them; and to say that London exhibits *only* a superficial likeness to Conrad obscures a basic correspondence which is of some significance in an over-all consideration of London's fiction. Consequently, I would like to examine here the nature and extent of London's relation to Conrad—not so much to determine Conrad's "influence" but rather to illuminate an infrequently considered aspect of London's work.

Certainly there can be no question of London's enthusiastic regard for Conrad. Mrs. London's record of the voyage of the *Snark* cites three occasions when Jack read Conrad aloud to the crew.[2] Frank Pease reported that London, while reading *A Personal Record,* exclaimed excitedly, "Here's Conrad saying a thing about a dog in two words that I've been trying to say all my life and couldn't."[3] The eponymous hero of *Martin Eden,* whose efforts to become a successful writer mirror the author's own early struggles (London remarked, "I was Martin Eden"), while composing what he considers his finest work makes the following appraisal: "There's only one man who could touch it... and that's Conrad. And it ought to make even him sit up and shake hands with me, and say, 'Well done, Martin, my boy!' " In 1915 upon reading *Victory,* London wrote an effusive letter to Conrad, commenting, "I had just begun to write when I read your first early work. I have... madly appreciated you and communicated my appreciation to my friends through all these years."[4]

[1]A letter written on March 7, 1923, printed in G. Jean-Aubry, *Joseph Conrad, Life and Letters* (London: William Heinemann, Ltd., 1927), II, 295.

[2]Charmian London, *The Log of the "Snark"* (New York: The Macmillan Co., 1915), p. 57 "Youth"; p. 80 "Typhoon"; and p. 160 "The End of the Tether."

[3]Pease, "Impressions of Jack London," *Seven Arts,* I (March, 1917), 528.

[4]Charmian London, *The Book of Jack London* (New York: The Century Co., 1921), II, 312.

At the age of twenty-three, then, London admired Conrad greatly; and he was still asserting this admiration the year before his death. London's affinity to Conrad indicated by these continuing expressions of respect is less explicitly illustrated on several levels in his work. At least once he appears to have borrowed from a Conrad story directly and extensively; moreover, the basic theme of two of his important books is one which recurs throughout Conrad's writing. These correspondences appear to me to be worth examining in some detail.

II

London's first story was published in January, 1899, and his 1915 letter to Conrad states that he began reading him about that time. Evidence of the impact of this reading on London is apparent in "In a Far Country," London's fifth story, which was published in June, 1899; for this story seems to be a close parallel of Conrad's "An Outpost of Progress," first published in *Tales of Unrest* the preceding year. Walter F. Wright has commented on the similarity of theme in London's "To Build a Fire" and "An Outpost of Progress," noting that London in the physical realm as Conrad in the mental "has illuminated the mystery of existence,"[5] as he portrays a civilized man freezing to death in the arctic wastes. Actually, the earlier "In a Far Country" is much closer to Conrad's story in the description of characters, as well as in situation and incidents.

In "An Outpost of Progress," "Two perfectly insignificant and incapable individuals," Carlier and Kayerts, are left in charge of a trading post on the upper reaches of an African river. Since their existence had been "only rendered possible through the high organization of civilized crowds," the isolation of this outpost and "the contact with pure unmitigated savagery, with primitive nature and primitive man, brings sudden and profound trouble." They gradually deteriorate morally, emotionally and physically, eventually one kills the other and then commits suicide. In London's story, two "ordinary" men, the "Incapables" London repeatedly terms them, rather than undertake a hazardous thousand-mile journey while the remainder of their party, choose to spend the winter in an abandoned cabin on a tributary of the Yukon. Weatherbee and Cuthfert, "hardened to the ruts in which they were created," find the "pressure of the altered environment is unbearable, and they chafe in body and spirit" as they "face the savage youth, the primordial simplicity of the North...." The story is a record of their quarrels, their concomitant disintegration. Finally each is successful in killing the other.

[5]Wright, *Romance and Tragedy in Joseph Conrad* (Lincoln, Nebraska: University of Nebraska Press, 1949), p. 134.

Not only are both pairs of characters isolated from civilization; their isolation is described in similar terms. The "outpost of progress" is surrounded by an "impenetrable bush that seemed to cut off the station from the rest of the world.... they felt themselves very much alone, when suddenly left unassisted to face the wilderness.... The river, the forest, all the great land throbbing with life, were a great emptiness.... The river seemed to come from nowhere and flow nowhither." London's characters find that "Everything in the Northland had the crushing effect... the solemn forest which seemed to guard an awful, inexpressible something...." Cuthfert comes to feel that "There was no Southland," for beyond the "bleak sky-line there stretched vast solitudes, and beyond these still vaster solitudes."

Early in "An Outpost of Progress" Kayerts and Carlier are seen through the eyes of the director of the company who comments to another employee as they leave the two at their post: "Look at those two imbeciles. They must be mad at home to send me such specimens.... I bet nothing will be done! They won't know how to begin." The "old stager" replies with a quiet smile, "They will form themselves here." Sloper, in charge of the party in London's story, having previously marked the incompetence of Weatherbee and Cuthfert, comments to Jacques Baptiste, a native of the Northland, as they leave the two standing in the doorway of the cabin: "Now, these two men don't like work. They won't work. We know that. They'll be all alone in that cabin all winter,—a mighty long, dark winter. Kilkenny cats, well?" Baptiste responds with "an eloquent shrug, pregnant with prophecy."

Finally, the events illustrating the demoralization of the two pairs of men coincide in the following particulars: at first all goes well, but since they are unsupervised they do nothing except what is essential and even routine tasks are slackly performed. None of the men is fitted to grapple with this situation and as the slow days pass they degenerate mentally and physically. The memory of civilization recedes and they become ill from the lack of fresh food, their appearance altering to the extent that, in a scene in both stories, each comes on the other suddenly and fails to recognize him. In both stories the characters achieve a virulent, unreasoning hatred for each other and finally quarrel fatally over the same thing, the supply of sugar. In fact, there is only one important stage of "An Outpost of Progress" that does not have a counterpart in London's tale: the increasing moral obliquity of Carlier and Kayerts as dramatized through their passive acceptance of the selling of some friendly natives into slavery.

It is difficult to say, of course, whether London consciously borrowed from Conrad's story. It is apparent, however, that both the situation and the theme of the two stories are the same and that the theme of "In a Far Country" is much closer to Conrad than that of any of London's previous stories. London had handled each of his first four stories ("To the Man on Trail," "The White Silence," "The Son of the Wolf," and "The Men of Forty-Mile") as a tour de force. An unusual situation in each instance brings one of the central characters to confront violence and perhaps death. But once London has delineated the situation, sketched the characters briefly and indicated the turn of action, the story is finished. "In a Far Country" also contains many of these elements. The theme, however, is not catastrophe (surmounted or not) but disintegration. "In a Far Country," like "An Outpost of Progress," goes beyond the description of nature, and of man trying to exist on the "natural" physical level: Two unexceptional men, neither particularly good or bad, placed in isolation in an unfamiliar and unfriendly environment, reach a point of complete moral and emotional as well as physical breakdown. London himself was aware that this story differed from his first four, for in May, 1899, he wrote his friend Cloudesley Johns

> I wonder what you will think of 'In a Far Country,' which comes out in the June Number [*Overland Monthly*] and which contains no reference to Malemute Kid or any other character which has previously appeared. As I recollect my own judgement of it, it is either bosh or good; either the worst or the best of the series I have turned out.[6]

It seems possible and even likely that London's recent discovery and "mad appreciation" of Conrad may have been partly responsible for his somewhat different attempt in this story.

III

A statement by Martin Eden points to a more revealing if less direct aspect of London's relation to Conrad. Eden is confident that he will merit Conrad's approval for

> beneath the swing and go of the story was to be something else.... it was always the great, universal motif that suggested plots to him. After having found such a motif he cast about for the particular persons and particular location in time and space wherewith and wherein to utter the universal thing.

In this book and in the later *John Barleycorn,* although London's presentation is much more personal, uncontrolled and fragmentary than Conrad's, the "universal thing" is a motif with which Conrad was much concerned, particularly in "Youth" and "Heart of Darkness": an individual's attempt to achieve self-identifying values in a tragic

[6]Charmian London, *The Book of Jack London,* I, 293.

and ironic universe. *Martin Eden* is usually said to be about a writer torn between working-class and bourgeois standards; and *John Barleycorn* is considered a semi-accurate autobiography giving principal stress to London's alcoholic experiences. A comparison of these two books with "Youth" and "Heart of Darkness" focuses attention on the fact that there is a level of meaning beneath their obvious statements.

It is not surprising that as late as 1907 London was reading "Youth" aloud to the crew of the *Snark*, for the characteristic tone of that story is of a part with the vigor of much of London's writing, his love of the sea and the zest for life which typified his young manhood.[7] The twenty-year-old Marlow and young Jack London in his autobiographical writings both feel that a glamorous life of romantic adventure at sea is unfolding before them, that each is on the verge of discovering his essential nature, and both experience the intoxicating sense of accomplishment of the youth just beginning to find himself. Marlow thrills to the thought of a voyage to the mysterious East, even in a "rattletrap" of a ship: "Youth and the sea. Glamour and the sea! The good, strong sea, the salt, bitter sea, that would whisper to you and roar at you and knock your breath out of you." On the voyage Marlow begins to discover himself, that he was only twenty and

> here I am lasting it out as well as any.... There was all the East before me, and a life, and the thought that I had been tried in that ship and had come out pretty well.... I did not know how good a man I was till then.... I remember my youth and... the feeling that I could last forever, outlast the sea, the earth, and all men....

A corresponding picture of youthful exuberance is presented in *Martin Eden* and *John Barleycorn.* To young Jack London in the latter book, "the winds of adventure" blew up and down San Francisco Bay where "the afternoon sea breeze blew its tang into my lungs, and curled the waves in mid-channel.... There it was, the smack and slap of the spirit of revolt, of adventure, of romance, of the things forbidden and done defiantly and grandly." Like Marlow, London is half apologetic about the actual facts of the adventure. "And now, of all this that is squalid, and ridiculous, and bestial, try to think what it meant to me, a youth not yet sixteen, burning with the spirit of adventure.... Came the whisper to range farther. I had not found it yet. There was more behind." Of course the themes of alcohol and lawlessness in *John Barleycorn* introduce some facets of youthful experi-

[7] Charmian London refers to "Youth" as "this masterpiece of which he [Jack] and I never tire, many times though we have read it." *The Log of the Snark,* p. 57.

ence with which Conrad does not deal, but for the most part these two aspects of London's life merely heighten the mood of adventure which permeates both "Youth" and the parts of *John Barleycorn* describing London's early life. In *Martin Eden* the experiences of the protagonist as a sailor are not stressed, but he has the same zest for experience, the same compulsion to realize his identity that the youthful Marlow has. The tone of the first part of the book is set by Martin's radiant enthusiasm as he discovers a new social and intellectual world. As he begins to feel at home in that world, his confidence in his own ability mounts. "He was profoundly happy. Life was pitched high. He was in a fever that never broke. The joy of creation that is supposed to belong to the gods was his." Slowly he begins to become aware that "The climb [to social and intellectual competence] had been easier than he expected. He was superior to the climb, and (he did not, with false modesty, hide it from himself) he was superior to the beings among whom he had climbed...."

In the first parts of these books then, London, like Conrad in "Youth," gives a vivid picture of the spiritually undefeated youth exulting in his new-found powers. But twenty-two years have passed and Marlow must now say, anticipating the more somber mood of "Heart of Darkness," that even while we are "looking anxiously for something out of life, that while it is expected is already gone—has passed unseen, in a sigh, in a flash—together with the youth, with the strength, with the romance of illusions.... Youth, strength, genius, thoughts, achievements, simple hearts—all die...." The central characters of *Martin Eden* and *John Barleycorn* have also experienced the passing of time, and the tone of the concluding portions of both books coincides with the tone of this statement and with the even darker expression of "Heart of Darkness."[8] In the conviction that "the so-called truths of life are not true," but are "illusions" by which one lives, the drunken protagonist of *John Barleycorn,* as he sinks into "fuddled sleep," recites "Yea, I am Youth because I die."

In comparing the sequential pictures of youth and disillusionment in Conrad and London there is some apparent difficulty since Conrad builds his study around a single character, one story illustrating each mood, and London deals with both moods in two works. Conrad, however, foreshadows "Heart of Darkness" in "Youth," and Marlow at the beginning of "Heart of Darkness" may be identified with the younger Marlow of the other story. Moreover, despite the fact that *Martin Eden* is a novel and *John Barleycorn* is avowedly

[8]Nowhere does London specifically mention "Heart of Darkness," but since it is the middle story of the volume also containing "Youth" and "The End of the Tether," both of which he read aloud on the *Snark* voyage, and since London admired Conrad so strongly, it seems certain that he did know it.

an autobiography, the books are closely related; for the former is based directly on London's experiences as a writer and the autobiography is often fictionalized with the result that the two together constitute a spiritual biography of the protagonist. *John Barleycorn,* written six years after *Martin Eden,* reinforces and supplements the characterization in the earlier work. The principal emphasis of *Martin Eden* falls on the hero's determined drive to fulfill himself,[9] to reach the social and economic class represented by the Morse family and to become a successful writer. The intensity of Martin's determination leaves little time for pessimism and even little time for the re-evaluation of his original goals. Only gradually does he discover that he will not find his true identity through the achievement of middle-class social status and financial success, that the goals which have given meaning to his existence for several years are paltry and stultifying: "He had hitched his wagon to a star and been landed in a pestiferous marsh." In the realization that neither he nor life had turned out to be what he had envisaged, he quickly succumbs to a mood of rather sophomoric despair and eventually commits suicide. This ending, of course, is not consonant with the first part of the book, and the reader is most likely to be confused by what has been called the ambiguous tone of the conclusion. London's purpose in *Martin Eden* is clarified by *John Barleycorn,* however. In the latter book there is still the apotheosis of individualistic striving to be found in *Martin Eden.* But in this book, despite the ostensible subject of alcoholism and despite London's extreme romanticization of his physical and intellectual exploits as a young man, the tone is not ambiguous. A substantial part of *John Barleycorn* is an amplification of the intellectual pessimism, of the self-dissatisfaction, of the despair which led Martin Eden to suicide.

When the two books are considered together, then, the pattern of experience which London has delineated is made clear. The progression has been from almost animal gusto to satiety, from the eager quest of experience to the center of indifference. Self knowledge has led to skepticism. Marlow's experience in "Heart of Darkness" is of the same pattern. At first he is a comparatively unreflecting young sailor, occupied with the world of "straightforward facts," eager for adventure. (Conrad remarked, "Before the Congo I was just a mere animal.") But Marlow-Conrad like Eden-London is led

[9]Such statements as "It was the first time he had ever really seen himself"; "he had learned much of himself"; "he had spent many hours in self analysis" occur throughout the book. These statements may be narcissism—they have been called that. The connotations evoked by this term, however, seem to me to obscure unnecessarily the fact that London, like Conrad in "Youth," has attempted to give a description of an exuberant, intelligent youth just discovering his own individuality.

to a reassessment of himself, of his values, of life itself; and this similar experience the two writers often describe in much the same terms.

By his experience on the African river and by his "loyalty" to Kurtz, Marlow is brought to the "ordeal of looking into myself," and he is thus led to the "threshold of the invisible":

> I have wrestled with death. It is the most unexciting contest you can imagine. It takes place in an impalpable grayness, with nothing underfoot, with nothing around, without spectators, without clamor, without glory, without the great desire of victory, without the great fear of defeat, in a sickly atmosphere of tepid skepticism, without much belief in your own right, and still less in that of your adversary.

London, during "this long sickness of pessimism... meditated suicide coolly," struggling in "the dusk of my soul" as he discourses with the White Logic which, under "a mask of hedonism," is the "Noseless One... whispering his whispers of death," and which "undefeated has never left me." "John Barleycorn sends his White Logic, the argent messenger of truth beyond truth, the antithesis of life, cruel and bleak as interstellar space, pulseless and frozen as absolute zero...."

Marlow does not die, but he does go through a period in which there is neither hope nor desire:

> I found myself back in the sepulchral city resenting the sight of people hurrying through the streets.... They trespassed upon my thoughts. They were intruders whose knowledge of life was to me an irritating pretense, because I felt so sure they could not possibly know the things I knew. Their bearing, which was simply the bearing of commonplace individuals going about their business... was offensive to me like the outrageous flauntings of folly in the face of a danger it is unable to comprehend. I had no particular desire to enlighten them, but I had some difficulty in restraining myself from laughing in their faces, so full of stupid importance.

London, too, during his "long sickness" turns from companionship:

> in the company of others I was driven to melancholy and spiritual tears. I could neither laugh with nor at the solemn utterances of men I esteemed ponderous asses.... [but] A cocktail, or several, before dinner, enabled me to laugh wholeheartedly at things which had long since ceased being laughable. ...[The cocktail] recrudesced the laughter and the song, and put a lilt into my own imagination so that I could laugh and sing and say... platitudes with verve and intensity to the satisfaction of the pompous mediocre ones who knew no other way to talk.

In a similar vein, Martin Eden finds it an increasing strain to be with people. Of the Morse family, he realizes

> The exalted beings he met there, and to whom he had looked up but a short time before, now bored him.... He was nervous and irritable...and the conversation of such people was maddening.... He measured the narrowness of their minds by the minds of the thinkers in the books he had read.... It was their ignorance that astounded him.

And he is also isolated from his former friends: "Their mode of life, which had once been his, was now distasteful to him.... He developed into an alien."

The level of experience as well as the respective attitudes of the two writers toward that experience, in these and similar passages, is manifestly different. Eden-London's "long sickness" is apparently in part the result of reading "too much positive science" and of a somewhat immature reaction to the fact that life had not turned out as he had wished—in contrast to Marlow's pessimism which seems to be the result of a sensitive and mature individual becoming aware, philosophically as well as emotionally, of the terrors of hell. London makes no attempt to use the traditional imagery and symbolism of the voyage to Hades which Conrad, like Virgil and Dante, employed "to create that otherwise formless region into which not only the artist but every man must descend if he wishes to understand himself."[10] And perhaps because of this very formlessness London's characters are less able to withstand their experience. Even so, London and Conrad in these works are writing about the same problem. Their characters achieve knowledge of themselves and their world, a knowledge which leads them to an awareness of man's capacity for and affinity to evil. This awareness is directly expressed by both authors in their frequent use of terms referring to physical and spiritual darkness. In the last two pages of "Heart of Darkness" the word *darkness* occurs five times; *black, dusk* and *somber* appear six. Marlow bows his head before the Intended's faith in Kurtz, "before that great and saving illusion that shone with an unearthly glow in the darkness, in the triumphant darkness from which I could not have defended her—from which I could not even defend myself." Martin Eden, close to suicide, expresses to Lizzie Connolly his need for a similar illusion: "You are a great and noble woman....And it is I who should be proud to know you.... You are a ray of light to me in a very dark world...." But nothing can save him, and one night as the "dark wall" of the ship rushes past, he lowers himself into the

[10]Lillian Feder, "Marlow's Descent into Hell," *Nineteenth-Century Fiction*, IX (March, 1955), 292.

Pacific. The concluding lines of the book describe his death. "There was a long rumble of sound, and it seemed to him that he was falling down a vast and interminable stairway. And somewhere at the bottom he fell into darkness. That much he knew. He had fallen into darkness." Conrad sets the final and characteristic mood of "Heart of Darkness" with this ending: "The offing was barred by a black bank of clouds, and the tranquil waterway leading to the uttermost ends of the earth flowed somber under an overcast sky—seemed to lead to the heart of an immense darkness."

This similarity of expression is made more emphatic by the almost identical summations of life made by the two writers. Marlow remarks: "Droll thing life is—that mysterious arrangement of merciless logic for a futile purpose." In *John Barleycorn* London says, "on every hand I see the merciless and infinite waste of natural selection. The White Logic insists upon opening the long-closed books, and... states the beauty and wonder I behold in terms of futility and dust." The "truths" here stated were, of course, in part the truths of all writers who contemplated the post-Darwinian cosmology from a certain point of view. Marlow confounds the beating of the savages' drum with the beating of his own heart; Eden's ambitions and reactions are principally shaped by his social environment. But neither writer in these books is unremittingly a naturalist, depicting his characters as animalistic drones rigidly controlled by biological and sociological forces. Although Marlow and Eden-London are confronted by these forces, the principal emphasis is on their *conscious* reaction to them. These protagonists consider that the world is a dark and futile place, but even as they investigate this insight they struggle with that darkness and futility. In these works London and Conrad coincide in differing from strict naturalists, for they both present the struggle from the side of the human antagonist. If one of London's "long-closed books" was "Heart of Darkness," he found a view of life fundamentally in keeping with the one he had expressed in the last parts of *Martin Eden* and *John Barleycorn.*

IV

That London admired Conrad greatly, that one story, "In a Far Country," can probably be traced directly to him, that London's view of life and at times the expression of that view, was somewhat similar to Conrad's is certainly not to say that London should be regarded literarily as "a son of Joseph Conrad." An extended comparison of these two writers quickly becomes a contrast which sharply emphasizes London's limitations as a prose writer and a thinker. London was a hack who refused to revise and referred to art as "consummate charlatanry"; he was a primordialist who wrote of brutal life, always "changing dogs into wolves and wolves into dogs"; and he was a social polemicist who hoped that by writing *The Iron Heel* he had "advanced the socialist cause by five minutes." Conrad was most certainly none of these.

In some instances, however, London is comparable to Conrad. By this partial comparison I have attempted to draw attention to the fact that although London wrote such potboilers as *Adventure* and is best remembered for such works as the stories of Alaska and *The Iron Heel,* there were times when he did not write out of sheer commercialism and also times when he did not write about primitive life or programs of collective action. There is some necessity for making this point; for London was so flagrantly a hack, so outspokenly a socialist, so redbloodedly a primordialist that there is a tendency to assume these terms completely define his work. Indeed, critics writing about *Martin Eden* and *John Barleycorn* find much the same elements that they discover in London's other work: Marx, Darwin, Nietzche and Mammon. These elements are obviously there, but there is also something else. In these two books London deals with the minds and values of his protagonists, with their experience of life in general, in a vein that at times approaches Conrad's.

Even though *Martin Eden* and *John Barleycorn* differ from London's "unique" contributions which brought him fame, wealth, notoriety and a place in literary histories, in some respects they must be considered the key books in an understanding of London and his fiction. On one level, these two most personal of London's books present a synthesis of the theories of socialism and raw individualism between which London vacillates throughout most of his work. To be sure, the protagonist in each is racked by his contradictory allegiances, but the focus of each book is on an individual in torment, not on conflicting ideologies. In presenting this individual whose values have disintegrated, London goes beyond a concern with social theory to make a final comment on life. Essentially this comment is—the horror. Underneath Martin Eden's dudgeon that he had been misunderstood, underneath London's insistence that the "long sickness" is behind him, it may be observed that to London socialism, individualism, materialism—nothing matters: the essential feature of these two books is the description of the youth full of zest for life who has become the adult without desire as he makes the debilitating self-discovery that he is hollow and his values are illusions.

London's treatment of his travail remains essentially loose and personal. There is too little of the conscious effort discernible in Conrad who, as Eliot has remarked of Shakespeare, "was occupied with the struggle—which alone constitutes life for a poet—to transmute his personal and private agonies into something rich and strange, something universal and impersonal." But in both *Martin Eden* and *John Barleycorn* the agony is there. Despite the aesthetic deficiencies of his portrayal, London, perhaps without being entirely aware that he was revealing himself so fully, has given a memorable portrait of the heart of darkness of a violent soul who is not only lost, but, knowing he is lost, has subsided into the hollow man. Moreover, even if the portrait were less effectively sketched than it is, it would be worth our attention; for London has given more than a picture of his own heart of darkness. Enmeshed as he was in the diverse forces making up the chaotic multiplicity of twentieth-century life, inevitably London described a spiritual wasteland not far removed from Marlow's, or Kurtz's—or even Eliot's.

Jack London was not to get a direct answer to the adulatory letter he wrote Conrad, Martin Eden did not get his desired accolade, for Conrad's reserve against London's verbal intemperance and his rigid adherence to artistic standards which exclude most of London's work inevitably made him chary of acknowledging even a distant kinship to the American writer. If we are to acquire an understanding of London's total attempt and achievement, however, we must eschew that reserve and that rigidity.

"The Kipling of the Klondike": Naturalism in London's Early Fiction

EARL WILCOX

London is often discounted in studies of American literature, and his place in the naturalistic writing of the late nineteenth and early twentieth century in America is often ignored. Professor Wilcox here explores the naturalistic elements found in the fiction London wrote after 1902. Three themes dominate, the concept of the survival of the fittest, determinism as a controlling element in the universe, and the ultimate superiority of the white man. In addition, London's treatment of women in these stories indicates his development of a new, stronger woman who can deal with the rigors of life in the North. Noteworthy especially is his treatment of Indian women who are almost always portrayed as being strong, loyal and courageous, a fact which seems to meliorate the racism or white superiority which appears in so many of London's works.

The first period of Jack London's fiction clearly indicates the ways in which both his personal experiences and his reading shaped his outlook. Though London had been writing and sending his stories to publishers for some time, not until December, 1899, when Houghton Mifflin offered him a contract for his first volume of short stories, did he gain any recognition. The first collection, *The Son of the Wolf* (1900), outlined the plots, introduced the characters, and announced the themes that were later to give London a title of which he was proud, "The Kipling of the Klondike." The stories tell of man's attempts to survive the forces of nature, the threat of savages, and the competition with other fortune seekers in the north country. In *The God of His Fathers* (1901) London was eager to show that he could vary his themes, though keeping them essentially the same as in the first collection: the survival of the fittest, the deterministic orientation of the universe, and the superiority of the inevitable white

Reprinted from *Jack London Newsletter,* VI (Jan.-April, 1973), pp. 1-12. Reprinted by permission of the editor.

man. In his first novel, *A Daughter of the Snows* (1902), London used his first opportunity to explore in some detail the ideas he had introduced in the short stories. When the novel proved an inept vehicle for London's talents at this point in his career, he turned again to the stories, exploring the same general theses in *Children of the Frost* (1902).

"The White Silence" introduced London's hero of the Yukon and the Klondike, the Malemute Kid. The story also introduced the dominant philosophical and stylistic patterns that characterize not only the stories and the novel of this first period of London's career but of the whole range of his fiction. Undoubtedly London's most secure position in American letters rests on the quality of these early stories. For in even the first one he shows his talent for developing a relationship between theme and character as he places man in the presence of the White Silence:

> The afternoon wore on, and with the awe, born out of the White Silence the voiceless travelers bent to their work. Nature has many tricks wherewith she convinces man of his finity,—the ceaseless flow of the tides, the fury of the storm, the shock of the earthquake, the long roll of heaven's artillery,—but the most tremendous, the most stupefying of all, is the passive phase of the White Silence. All movement ceases, the sky clears, the heavens are as brass; the slightest whisper seems sacrilege, and man becomes timid, affrighted at the sound of his own voice. Sole speck of life journeying across the ghostly wastes of a dead world he trembles at his audacity, realizes that his is a maggot's life, nothing more. Strange thoughts arise unsummoned, and the mystery of all things strives for utterance. And the fear of death, of God, of the universe, comes over him,—yearning for immortality, the vain striving of the imprisoned essence,—it is then, if ever, man walks along with God.[1]

This description of environment is significant primarily because London's naturalistic heroes must cope with it in order to survive. The interrelationship between man and nature is of central importance in London's fiction, even as it had been in Crane's *Maggie* where the city overcomes Maggie. For as Darwinian "animals," the characters in London's northland stories learn that they must adapt to the environment or be subdued by it. This relationship is clearly outlined in the beginning of "In a Far Country."

> When a man journeys into a far country, he must be prepared to forget many things he has learned, and to acquire such customs as are inherent with existence in the new land; he must abandon the old ideals and the old gods and often-

[1]Jack London, *Best Short Stories of Jack London* (New York: Garden City Books, 1953), p. 13.

> times he must reverse the very codes by which his conduct has hitherto been shaped. To those who have the protean faculty of adaptability, the novelty of such change may even be a source of pleasure; but to those who happen to be hardened to the ruts in which they were created, the pressure of the altered environment is unbearable, and they chafe in body and in spirit under the new restriction which they do not understand. This chafing is bound to act and react, producing diverse evils and leading to various misfortunes. It were better for the man who cannot fit himself to the groove, to return to his own country; if he delay too long, he will surely die.[2]

As a prelude to an "inevitable" battle between the Red Man and the White Man in a later story in the same collection, a similar setting in all its naturalistic splendor is detailed:

> On every hand stretched the forest primeval,—the home of noisy comedy and silent tragedy. Here the struggle for survival continued to wage with all its ancient brutality. Briton and Russian were still to overlap in the Land of the Rainbow's End—and this was the very heart of it—nor had Yankee good yet purchased its vast domain.
>
> The wolf-pack still clung to the flank of the cariboo herd, singling out the weak and the big with calf, and pulling them down as remorselessly as were it a thousand thousand generations into the past. The sparse aborigines still acknowledged the rule of their chiefs and medicine men, drove out bad spirits, burned their witches, fought their neighbors, and ate their enemies with a relish which spoke well of their bellies. But it was at the moment when the stone age was drawing to a close. Already, over unknown trails and chartless wilderness, were the harbingers of the steel arriving,—fair-faced, blue-eyed, indomitable men, incarnations of the unrest of their race. By accident or design, single-handed and in two and threes, they came from no one knew whither, and fought, or died, or passed, no one knew whence.[3]

The Darwinian concept of survival of the fittest is carefully woven into this pattern of man's struggles. In no less than ten of the first twenty-five stories the survival motif dominates the action, and it is implicit in almost all of the others. Although in later stories and a novel London was to expand the survival thesis to include species generally, in these first stories the emphasis primarily is that of survival of the individual.

In "The White Silence" Malemute accompanies a man and his wife through the Yukon in an attempt to get to civilization before

[2]Jack London, *The Call of the Wild, The Cruise of the Dazzler, And Other Stories of Adventure* (New York: Platt and Munk, 1960), p. 452.

[3]Jack London, *The God of His Fathers* (New York: McClure, Phillips, Co., 1902), pp. 1-2.

spring. But the hostile environment overcomes Mason, the traveler, in the form of a huge tree which falls on him. Nature plays the same trick on a group of travelers in "In a Far Country." Some of the voyageurs make the trip safely back to civilization, but two men from the "older" civilization remain behind and fail to survive because of their inability to adapt to the environment.

In these stories London makes clear that the "law of survival" permeates all levels of existence. For when Malemute's dogs weaken in their traces, the stronger dogs devour the weak. And when the dogs are unable to subsist on their own ration, they turn to men in order to survive. After Mason dies, Malemute tries to find food for himself and the woman, only to return to discover the dogs attacking. Darwinian survival is stated in its simplest terms.

> Bursting into the camp . . . (Malemute) saw the girl in the midst of the snarling pack, laying about her with an ax. The dogs had broken the iron rule of their masters and were rushing the grub. He joined the issue with his rifle reversed, and the hoary game of natural selection was played out with all the ruthlessness of its primeval environment. Rifle and ax went up and down, hit or missed with monotonous regularity; lithe bodies flashed, with wild eyes and dripping fangs; and men and beast fought for supremacy to the bitterest conclusion. Then the beaten brutes crept to the edge of the firelight, licking their wounds, voicing their misery to the stars.[4]

Indeed, only the fittest survive either nature's or man's attacks.

The affinity between man and dog is no mere accidental relationship to suggest that both obey laws of survival. In the evolutionary scheme of things both obey such laws because both are part of the evolutionary process. Man is merely a higher-order animal, and his survival, his progress toward a higher state, is dependent upon his adaptability. In the northland, environmental and hereditary traits are more forcefully evident because of the heightened struggle. And under stress, man shows his latent animal traits—his atavism—and reverts to that state. The allusion to "son" in "The Son of the Wolf" is probably meant, therefore, to convey that Scruff Mackenzie, the protagonist, is a descendant of some earlier animal form, or simply that his survival indicates his animal nature. London describes Mackenzie as a true product of the wild:

> Scruff Mackenzie bore the ear-marks of a frontier birth and a frontier life. His face was stamped with twenty-five years of incessant struggle with Nature in her wildest moods—the law too, the wildest and hardest of all having been spent in

[4]London, *Best Short Stories,* p. 7.

> groping for the gold which lies in the shadow of the Arctic Circle.[5]

The survival-oriented plot involves Mackenzie's desire to have Zarinska, an Indian maiden, for his wife. To win her he must fight Fox, the medicine man, who has been claiming that his black magic can subdue the white man's. Finally the two engage in physical battle in a fight for survival. The entire fight is a re-enactment of the survival motif:

> Time and again... (Mackenzie) was forced from the edge of the fire to the deep snow, and time again, with the foot tactics of the pugilist, he worked back to the centre. Not a voice was lifted in encouragement, while his antagonist was heartened with applause, suggestions, and warnings. (*Ibid.*, p. 45)

And in the final stages of the struggle, when Mackenzie is winning, the true son of the wolf emerges:

> At first he felt compassion for his enemy; but this fled before the primal instinct of life, which in turn gave way to the lust of slaughter. The ten thousand years of culture fell from him; and he was a cave-dweller, doing battle for his female. (*Ibid.*, pp. 45-46)

The atavism in Mackenzie is yet a latent characteristic of the "civilized" man. Precisely the same theory is propounded in the death of the two survivors in "In a Far Country," for when at last they have been overcome by the White Silence (environment) their true nature is evident: "What with the Fear of the North, the mental strain, the ravages of the disease, they lost all semblance of humanity, taking on the appearance of wild beasts, hunted and desperate."[6] Thus the survival tendency is pictured as inherent, as animal instinct. The implicit materialism in this view of a biological assumption is the central idea also in "Jan, the Unrepentant" in the same collection. Having been found guilty of killing a man, Jan flees, and during the pursuit his instinct for survival seems to give him courage:

> Jan ran blindly, reckoning not of the way of his feet, for he was mastered by the verb "to live." To live. To exist. Buck flashed gray through the air, but missed. The man struck madly at him, and stumbled. Then the white teeth of Bright closed on his mackinaw jacket, and he pitched into the snow. *To live! To exist!* He fought wildly as ever, the centre of a tossing heap of men and dogs. (*Ibid.*, p. 347).

[5]Jack London, *The Son of the Wolf, Tales of the Far North* (New York: Arco Publications, 1962), p. 28.

[6]London, *Stories of Adventure,* p. 452.

This ubiquitous survival thesis takes on protean forms in London's early stories. For examples, not only is man forced to do battle with nature, with animals, with other white men to survive, the Red Man also provides added challenge. Though the Red Man-White Man encounters are given trite portrayal in London's stories, the central significance is in providing for another dimension of the survival themes. In "God of His Fathers," whose setting we have noted earlier, the struggle is intensely dramatized in a familiar naturalistic pattern. Hay Stockard, a white man, hopes to live in the Yukon. But his arch-enemy, Baptiste the Red (an Indian), will not let him, primarily because Baptiste wants Stockard to admit that there is no God. An open struggle is precipitated by the appearance of Sturges Owen, a missionary priest. Stockard, married to an Indian girl who is now the mother of his child, and Baptiste are continuing their debate when Owen arrives. Baptiste refuses to let Owen preach to him, though he is willing for the priest to pass safely through the country. Owen is adamant: he will stay and preach to the "heathen." Though he despises Owen, Stockard vacillates between his desire to let the priest be killed and his inclination to help defend him against Baptiste. It is Owen, the cowardly priest, whom London disparages, for in the battle—a futile one in which the wife, the child, and several others are killed—Owen muses on his materialistically-oriented impulse to live in the knowledge of the martyrdom he could achieve. There is little that is admirable in Owen's death; in fact, the story's ending seems to imply that the priest has been foolish in dying for a cause which apparently means very little to him except as it will bring him some personal glory.

The most original aspect of the struggle between the White Man and the Red Man as introduced in these first stories is London's belief in the superiority of the White, Anglo-Saxon race. This thesis, which is a dominant and pervasive one in all of London's later fiction, is proclaimed as part of the survival theory. While not Darwinian in origin, the theory is at least Darwinistic, stressing the survival of the species as it adapts to its environment. Scruff Mackenzie, the son of the wolf, is the first character in London's fiction to voice the belief in white supremacy. After Mackenzie has won his mate, he proudly proclaims that his "people... are the mightiest of all the peoples, who rule all the lands...."[7] And the corollary law of the wolf is "whoso taketh the life of one wolf, the forfeit shall ten of his people pay." (*Ibid.*)

While the theme is merely hinted at in Mackenzie's brief statement, London uses one entire story to focus on his concept. In "The

[7]London, *The Son of the Wolf,* p. 44.

Great Interrogation" Karen Sayther is London's spokesman for the "new" civilization, for the Anglo-Saxon. Ostensibly Mrs. Sayther has left a comfortable estate in the city to come to the Yukon on an unknown errand. The "interrogation" into which the citizens of the territory are drawn is in wondering why Karen has come. It is shortly revealed that before her sudden marriage to the late Colonel Sayther, Karen had been engaged to David Paine, the hero of the story. She has returned to persuade David to return to civilization with her. He now lives with an Indian maiden and is caught in the matrix of deciding between the two ways of life. He recognizes that Karen has earlier deserted him for Colonel Sayther's money: the materialistic ideals of civilization were evident in the Colonel. Paine thinks of this, wondering, "What was he? A great, gross, material creature, deaf to song, blind to beauty, dead to the spirit. He was fat with laziness, and flabby-cheeked, and the round of his belly witnessed his glutony—."[8] But Karen dismisses David's charges and pleads with him on the basis of their anthropological ties.

> Come, Dave, you must see. She (Winapie the Indian girl) is not your kind. There is no race affinity. She is an aborigine, sprung from the soil, yet close to the soil, and impossible to live from the soil. Born savage, savage she will die. But we—you and I—the dominant, evolved race, the salt of the earth and the masters thereof: We are made for each other. The supreme call is of kind, and we are of kind. Reason and feeling dictate it. Your very instinct demands it. That you cannot deny. You cannot escape the generations behind you. Yours is an ancestry which has survived for a thousand centuries, and for a hundred thousand centuries, and your line must not stop here. It cannot. Your ancestry will not permit it. Instinct is stronger than the will. The race is mightier than you. Come, Dave, let us go. (*Ibid.*, pp. 56-57)

David then considers the alternatives, civilization or the primitive North:

> His bleak life rose up and smote him,—the vain struggle with pitiless force; the dreary years of frost and famine; the harsh and jarring contact with elemental life; the aching void which mere animal existence could not fill. And there, seduction by his side, whispering of brighter, warmer land, of music, light, and joy, called the old times back again. He visioned it unconsciously. Faces rushed in upon him; glimpses of forgotten scenes, memories of merry hours; strains of songs and trills of laughter—.
>
> "Come, Dave, Come," Karen said. "I have for both. The way is soft."

[8]London, *The God of His Fathers,* pp. 52-53.

> She was in his arms, trembling, and he held her tightly. He rose to his feet.... But the snarling hungry dogs, and the shrill cries of Winapie bringing about peace between the combatants, came muffled to his ear through the heavy logs. And another scene flashed before him. A struggle in the forest,—a bald-face grizzly broken-legged, terrible; the snarling of the dogs and the shrill cry of Winapie as she urged them to the attack; himself in the midst of the crush, breathless, panting, striving to hold off red death; broken-backed, entrail-ripped dogs howling in impotent anguish and desecrating the snow; the virgin white running scarlet with the blood of man and beast; the bear, ferocious, irresistible, crunching, crunching down to the core of his life.... (*Ibid.,* p. 57)

While the final outcome of the story argues not for a victory for the "dominant, evolved race" (since David chooses not to return with Karen), London still asserts that the Anglo-Saxon species has evolved to its superiority through its struggle for survival. In a later story in *Children of the Frost,* written in this first period of his career also, London pictures Avery Von Brunt as he nears an Indian village with the same Anglo-Saxon consciousness: "He, alone, was full-blooded Saxon, and his blood was pounding fiercely through his veins to the traditions of his race. Clive and Hastings, Drake and Raleigh, Hengest and Horsa, walked with him."[9]

But Jack London is not content with asserting the white supremacy through the voice of his white men; he must also depict the Red Man's coming to the same conclusion. Thus the "Law of Life" for an old Indian chieftain, Koskoosh, is that a Darwinian biological concept explains the way of all flesh and the evils visited upon it. In a resigned mood of despair, Koskoosh laments his defeat:

> It was the law of all flesh. Nature was not kindly to the flesh. She had no concern for that concrete thing called the individual. Her interest lay in the species, the race. This was the deepest abstraction Old Koskoosh's barbaric mind was capable of, but he grasped it firmly. He saw it exemplified in all life. The rise of the sap, the bursting greenness of the willow bud, the

[9]Jack London, *Children of the Frost* (London: Arco Publications, 1963), pp. 12-13. Except for Taine's almost metaphorical assertion of the superiority of the French, no other naturalist has asserted a similar theory. Indeed, the American naturalists were wont to demonstrate that the human species was in no way superior to other species, that man was merely an animal of a higher order. London also preaches this simple biological theory time and time again. Thus his attempts to assert on the one hand a racial superiority and on the other an implicit atavism not only confuse his philosophy but also necessitate a stricter qualification of the degree of London's affinity with the naturalistic movement. If London's use of the concept is to be considered naturalistic, one feels that he is on the periphery of the movement rather than in the mainstream. The only justification that can be made for inclusion of the motif here is on the basis of London's belief that the Anglo-Saxon race had evolved through centuries of struggle to become the dominant race. Aside from the fiction, see his statements in the *Kempton-Wace Letters* (p. 9, 54). See also Joan London's reports of the numerous occasions in which her father discussed his race views.

> fall of the yellow leaf—in this alone was told the whole history. (*Ibid.*, p. 33)

The "law" is, of course, the "natural" law of the white man's supremacy. Another grand old chieftain comes to precisely the same conclusion about natural selection. In "The League of Old Men," Imber tells a white man's court of his attempts to eradicate the white man before he destroyed Imber's civilization. In the end Imber's people are defeated, for it is the "Anglo-Saxon who have the custom of... giving the law to conquered peoples, and oft-times this law is harsh." (*Ibid.*, p. 143) At last unable to fight because of his age, Imber has come to the city to tell his story and to acknowledge the "law." He laments, "I am very old, and very tired, and it being vain fighting the Law, as thou sayest.... I am come seeking the Law." (*Ibid.*, pp. 159-160) The white man's law fuses again with the laws of nature in Imber's dim mind as he sits in rapturous contemplation of the inevitable forces that control his life:

> But Imber was dreaming. The square-browed judge likewise dreamed and all his race rose up before him in a mighty phantasmagoria—his steel-shod mail-clad race, the law-giver and world-maker among the families of men. He saw it dawn red-flickering across the dark forests and sullen seas; and he saw it blaze, bloody and red, to full and triumphant noon; and down the shaded slope he saw the blood-red sands dropping into night. And through it all he observed the Law, pitiless and potent, ever unswerving and ever ordaining, greater than the motes of men who fulfllled it or were crushed by it, even as it was greater than he, his heart speaking for softness. (*Ibid.*, p. 160)

In these stories London asserts the Kiplingesque myth of the superior White Race, but he also adapts it to a naturalistic framework. For the survival thesis is clearly Darwinian in import. Too, the tone in which the survival and natural selection principles are adumbrated is obviously naturalistic. In "The Men of Forty Mile," for example, London explains that life in general is explainable in terms of a deterministic framework. In the story the same Scruff Mackenzie is a central figure in a brief struggle with another white man. It is the Malemute Kid, however, who glibly voices a naturalistic assumption in noting that men should understand that life itself is a gamble, a kind of game with no predictable outcome. Thus after attempting unsuccessfully to settle an argument between two men, the Kid concludes: "So you see we do not actually take away the privilege of fighting; and yet I don't believe they'll fight when they see the beauty of the scheme. Life's a game, and men the gamblers."[10] Furthermore,

[10]London, *Stories of Adventure*, p. 480.

London adheres to the technique he has outlined before when in the same stories he depicts the Indians expressing the same kind of pessimism in reacting to a deterministic pattern of survival. Sitka Charley, the Indian hero who appears in many of the tales of this early period, tells of his taking a long journey with a white man and woman. Ostensibly, the story is about "The Grit of Woman," but it finally develops into a philosophical soliloquy in which Charley muses on the deterministic orientation of the universe. The plot, a typical one for London, concerns a white man's great love for his Indian squaw and their many years of hardship in the north. But the couple is finally to be defeated by nature, and the narrative centers around their demise, described in language reminiscent of the meaning of "The White Silence." In the story both the hero and his wife are overcome—by their environment. But before the narrator dies, he asserts the pessimist's creed: life, which must be viewed materialistically, is futile and meaningless:

> Life is a strange thing. Much have I thought on it, and pondered long, yet daily the strangeness of it grows not less, but more. Why this longing for Life? It is a game which no man wins. To live is to toil hard, and to suffer sore, till Old Age creeps heavily upon us and we throw down our hands on the ashes of dead forest. It is hard to live. In pain the babe sucks his first breath, in pain the old man gasps his last and all his days are full of trouble and sorrow; yet he goes down to the open arms of Death, stumbling, falling, with head turned backward, fighting, to the last. And Death is kind. It is only Life, and the things of Life that hurt. Yet we love Life, and we hate Death.[11]

What is not accomplished in Charley's statement is captured in fuller measure in the clearest philosophical statement of determinism in the early stories. Like Malemute Kid's earlier declaration that life is a game, Fortune La Perle, the protagonist of "Which Make Men Remember," comes to the same pessimistic conclusion. Fortune, who is accused of murdering John Randolphe, is befriended by Uri Bram. Uri hides Fortune from authorities, and while spending the many days waiting to come out of hiding, the outlaw meditates on his destiny. Obviously allegorizing the man's name for thematic impact, London portrays Fortune as feeling that

> Life is a skin-game, chance. I was faked in my birth and flim-flammed with my mother's milk. The dice were loaded when she toed the boz, and I was born to prove the loss. (*Ibid.*, p. 75)

[11]London, *The God of His Fathers*, pp. 176-177. London's pessimism sprang from multiple sources, part of which was genuine and part of which was a literary device in imitation of Schopenhauer.

Fortune's own account of how he came to murder Randolphe is enunciated in classic deterministic terms:

> All worked out, every bit of it, all parts fitting snug. Before I was born, like as not. I'll put the sack I never hope to get on it, before I was born. That's why. (*Ibid.,* p. 83)

Finally, Uri and Fortune decide to draw cards to see who will shoot first in a duel through which Bram seeks to revenge his friend, Randolphe. London, the naturalistic cynic, disparaging traditional Christian concepts, shows his cynicism in arranging the unusual denouement in which Bram seeks the revenge. The duel is set, with long ardent statements from Bram on the virtues of justice and on the virtues of his friend Randolphe whose great name must be avenged. But Fortune's god is quite different from Bram's: "He did not know much concerning Uri's God, but he believed in Chance." And as they draw cards, Fortune feels that surely "Chance (will) not desert him now." The narrator (London) tells the reader, "Chance had been very good to him (Fortune) already . . . and if he tricked now he would have to pay for it afterward." (*Ibid.*, p. 84) But Fortune loses the draw and is killed. As he dies, the fatalist succumbs amid London's refrain: "Fortune did not whirl, but gay San Francisco dimmed and faded: and as the sun-bright snow turned blacker and blacker, he breathed his last malediction on the Chance he had misplayed." (*Ibid.*, p. 85)

The women in London's early stories constitute an integral part of the total view of life in the northland. Not insignificantly London's first novel, also written during this period, centers around a woman. Because of the encompassing manner in which London explores the many avenues through which his naturalism can be expressed, he was wise not to discard the role of woman in these adventure tales. Importantly, then, a superior type of woman is needed to cope with the rigorous life demanded by the environment. A review of the tales already discussed indicates that the role of woman is a central one. In "The White Silence" the woman successfully fights off the pack until Malemute returns; in "The Son of the Wolf" Scruff's squaw is pictured as a sturdy and courageous woman; in "The God of His Fathers" the Indian wife of Stockard gladly dies for her white husband; in "The Great Interrogation" David Paine chooses to remain in the wilderness with his Indian maiden; and in "The Grit of Women" the courage and fidelity of women are emphasized. It may be noted parenthetically that London's alleged disdain for the Red Man is not borne out in a reading of these early stories. The Indian women, particularly, are consistently presented in a courageous and honorable light. Not unexpectedly, then, London advances a theory which also exalts the heroism of a white woman. In the "Priestly Prerogative" his first naturalistic "new woman" enters the scene. In the story, the "new woman" is Grace Bentham. Grace, the wife of Edwin Bentham, has come with her husband to the Yukon territory. Both have been reared in the city and thus are tenderfeet, until Grace sees that in order to survive she must take charge of the family affairs. Eventually, by Grace's clever maneuvering of their money, her buying of land, and her strict urging and directing Edwin to push farther north, the couple emerge wealthy. The "new woman" motif is announced in London's description of Grace's efficiency:

> This was the woman who urged her husband in his Northland quest, who broke trail for him when no one was looking, and cried in secret over her weakling woman's body. So journeyed this strangely assorted couple down to old Fort Selkirk, then through five-score miles of dismal wilderness to Stuart River. And when the short day left them, and the man lay down in the snow and blubbered, it was the woman who lashed him to the sled, bit her lips with the pain of her aching limbs, and helped the dog haul him to Malemute Kid's cabin.[12]

Her greatest energies are then directed in earning a fortune for them:

> This is what Grace Bentham proceeded to do. Arriving in Dawson with a few pounds of flour and several letters of introduction, she at once applied herself to the task of pushing her big baby to the fore. It was she who melted the stony heart and wrung credit from the rude barbarian who presided over the destiny of the P. C. Company.... It was she who studied maps, catechised miners, and hammered geography and locations into his hollow head, till everybody marvelled at his broad grasp of the country and knowledge of its conditions....
>
> She did the work; he got the credit and reward. (*Ibid.*)

The "priestly prerogative" is made by a priest in the camp who discovers that Grace is in love with a close friend of the Benthams and plans to leave the Yukon country with him. The priest decides not to tell Edwin, assuring Grace that if she returns and remains faithful to Edwin her secret will always remain with her confessor. In general, the story epitomizes the materialistic aims which all the big fortune-seekers had in coming to the Yukon. Their lives, their hearts, and their souls are at stake in their desire to become rich and to "survive" on a larger scale than their neighbors. Yet the kind of survival which Jack London explores in these early stories was expressed primarily in terms of animal instinct, with an occasional hint of race survival, both views stressing that the species was strengthened by the emer-

[12]London, *The Son of the Wolf,* p. 99.

gence of the winner. In the study of Grace Bentham, London indicates his early fascination with the strong, Amazon-like woman who became one of his dominant character types in the later novels.

Henry S. Commager has well noted London's characteristic position in these early stories, as well as in much of the later fiction:

> Of all those who applied the doctrine of the survival of the fittest to human society, Jack London was the most enthusiastic and the most naive; it is suggestive that he was, also, the most widely read, at home and abroad.... London translated Darwin into the vernacular, presented it in a guise so romantic, boisterous, and extravagant that it proved irresistible; he wrote it up in dime novels and purveyed it as literature and philosophy. The stuff of his endless adventure stories was dredged up from his own fabulous career as newsboy, oyster pirate, tramp, sailor, prospector, and rancher; the philosophy was laid on like ornamental scrollwork on Eastlake buildings. London read Spencer and Haeckel and took the struggle for existence to be but a prophecy of his own struggle with the thugs of the San Francisco waterfront; he read Nietzsche and imagined himself a Superman. Science and philosophy conspired to explain his career and justify his fiction.[13]

To make these first stories superior in artistry, London buttressed both action and philosophical comment with a setting that complemented the tone and theme. Thus they achieve coherence and meaning despite Commager's claim that the philosophy is ornamental. What these stories portend is a pattern of naturalistic thought that permeates the greater part of all of Jack London's writing after 1902.

[13]Henry S. Commager, *The American Mind* (New Haven: Yale University Press, 1950), p. 110.

A New Reading of *The Sea Wolf*

JAMES ELLIS

To many readers, The Sea Wolf *embodies the basic conflict which permeates London's works, the conflict between the brute and the civilized man. The brute, Wolf Larson, is threatened by the idealism of Humphrey Van Weyden and Maud Brewster and must come to grips with that conflict just as many of London's other characters do. Many readers, however, are inaccurate in their assessment of Larson, seeing him only as the brute and ignoring the effects of the aesthetic and intellectual influence brought to him by Hump and Maud. Professor Ellis illuminates this side of Larson and defines the novel's central conflict as Larson's attempt to refute these humanizing influences. Larson's physical deterioration is the indication of the failure of the brute in him to overcome these other forces.*

Very soon after publication of *The Sea Wolf,* Ambrose Bierce wrote a critique of the novel, which reads in part:

> It is a most disagreeable book, as a whole. London has a pretty bad style and no sense of proportion. The story is a perfect welter of disagreeable incidents. Two or three (of the kind) would have sufficed to show the character of the man Larsen. . . .[1]

Bierce's suggestion that Larsen's character is in microcosm a "disagreeable incident" has been generally endorsed by the few subsequent critics who have written on *The Sea Wolf.*[2]

[1]In a letter to George Sterling, February 18, 1905. Quoted in Philip S. Foner, *Jack London: American Rebel* (New York, 1947), pp. 61-62.

[2]For Robert Spiller, Larsen is the "amoral superman...[who] knows only the primitive law of survival through predatory ruthlessness..." *Literary History of the United States* (New York, 1960), p. 1036. Alfred Kazin sees Larsen as a "primitive" hero who expresses London's desperate love of violence and its undercurrent of romanticism..." *On Native Grounds* (Garden City, New York, 1956), p. 87. Similarly, Charles Walcutt finds that Larsen recognizes "no values of laws, but those of his own life-impulse or 'will' [and] acts upon a program of complete selfishness" *American*

It is true that London gives to Larsen many speeches which suggest the brute. For example, Larsen in an oft-quoted passage tells Hump:

> "I believe that life is a mess.... It is like yeast, a ferment, a thing that moves and may move for a minute, an hour, a year, or a hundred years, but that in the end will cease to move. The big eat the little that they may continue to move, the strong eat the weak that they may retain their strength. The lucky eat the most and move the longest, that is all."[3]

This speech, however, represents only a partial view of Wolf Larsen and fails to account for the complexity of the man.

Complex Larsen certainly is, for though he glories in his primacy upon the miniature floating world of the *Ghost*, he is anything but at peace with himself and his world. Rather like Hamlet (who Van Weyden tells us is Larsen's favorite Shakespearean character) Larsen is disgusted with his world. He judges it as "piggishness" and asks: " 'Of what use or sense is an immortality of piggishness?' " Larsen, furthermore, makes even more explicit his dissatisfaction with life. Citing *Ecclesiastes,* he says:

> "For the Preacher loved life, and did not want to die, saying, 'For a living dog is better than a dead lion.' He preferred the vanity and vexation to the silence and the unmovableness of the grave. And so I. To crawl is piggish; but not to crawl, to be as the clod and rock, is loathsome to contemplate. It is loathsome to the life that is in me, the very essence of which is movement, the power of movement. Life itself is unsatisfaction, but to look ahead to death is greater unsatisfaction" (p. 76).

While Wolf Larsen can judge his materialistic world as "piggish" and "unsatisfaction," he can at the same time ecstatically rejoice at the natural beauty to be found in the world. In that passage early in the novel when both Hump and Larsen are presented captivated by the effect of the trade winds upon the schooner (in Hump's words, "the unending glory of what I never dreamed the world possessed"), Larsen tells Hump:

> "Do you know. I am filled with a strange uplift; I feel as if all time were echoing through me, as though all powers were mine. I know truth, divine good from evil, right from wrong. My vision is clear and far. I could almost believe in God" (p. 54).

Literary Naturalism, A Divided Stream (Minneapolis, 1956), p. 107. Finally, Maxwell Geismar judges Larsen "a cruel and to a large degree corrupt natural man' " *Rebels and Ancestors* (Boston, 1953), p. 153.

[3] Jack London, *The Sea Wolf,* ed. Matthew J. Bruccoli (Boston, 1964), p. 37. Subsequent references will be incorporated into the text and will refer to this edition.

Larsen's exclamation reveals an idealistic and aesthetic aspect of him which is the same as that which caused him to judge the world as "piggish." It would seem then that to view Wolf Larsen as complete unto himself (the strongest brute in a brutal world) is to overlook both his disgust for his materialism and the joy that he derives from beauty. It is within this complex ambiguity of Wolf Larsen that the meaning of the novel resides.

During the voyage of the *Ghost*, the aesthetic Humphrey Van Weyden and the materialistic Wolf Larsen enter into a form of *Doppelgänger* relationship. As "doubles," each tutors the other with the result that Hump comes to see the realities of the material world and Larsen to confront those of the spiritual. That this relationship of the "double" exists can be substantiated by noting how carefully London developed the changing roles of Hump and Larsen. In the beginning of the novel as Hump drifts alone in the fog after the *Martinex* has been sunk, it is Wolf Larsen himself who sights him, meets his eyes with his own, and then thrusts the helmsman aside so as to be able himself to bring his ship around. Moreover, in addition to the question of why Larsen rescues Hump (he literally and symbolically raises Hump from the dead) is the still more puzzling question of why the materialistic Larsen refuses Hump's offer of a thousand dollars to return him to the mainland. Further, Larsen elevates Hump to the position of the dead mate (Johansen), and Hump comes to temporary command of the *Ghost* when Larsen is below with his headaches. And finally at the end of the novel, the device of the "double" is given its logical conclusion with Larsen's and Hump's exchanging of roles—Hump becoming master of the *Ghost* through usurpation, and Wolf Larsen, dying and being buried in the same sea from which he had rescued Hump. We can assume then a relationship between the two men that deserves to be taken as of more than ordinary significance.

It is after Larsen has revealed his two sides to Hump, one materialistic and the other aesthetic, that Hump comes upon Larsen in the privacy of his cabin with his "head buried in his hands and his shoulders... heaving convulsively as with sobs." Hump says:

> He seemed torn by some mighty grief. As I softly withdrew I could hear him groaning, "God! God! God!" Not that he was calling upon God; it was mere expletive, but it came from his soul (p. 69).

I suggest that the result of Wolf Larsen's association with Hump is this onslaught of headaches (which Larsen says are new to him, he never having been sick or suffered from headaches before), and that these headaches symbolize a tension in Larsen between his intellectual allegiance to a materialistic world and his aesthetic sense of the impossibility of living joyfully in such a world.[4] He is, in short, a man who in his hubris cannot believe in (though he feels himself respond to) an irrational and unknowable truth of the heart that values idealism more than life itself. That these headaches do in fact symbolize this fragmenting of Larsen is supported by the fact that they begin to occur only after Hump has been brought on board and has become the confidant of Wolf Larsen.[5]

The entrance of Maud Brester into the world of the *Ghost* is London's device for procuring a final confrontation between Hump and Larsen and for developing the tension within Larsen that has arisen as a result of his bringing Hump into his world. No sooner does Maud come on board than Hump assumes the role of her protector and Larsen begins to pay suit to her. The result of this triangle is a maneuvering by which Hump and Maud seek to escape Larsen's brutality and Larsen to understand and thereby to destroy these two literati. Yet Larsen finds that the end of his scornful probing of Hump and Maud is not, as he had imagined, the abject collapse of their idealism before the reasoned attack of his materialism, but instead the calling down upon his own head of what Hump terms the "old primal melancholy."

In the company of Maud and Hump, Wolf Larsen laments the happiness he observes in them, saying: " 'You must be happy, you sentimentalists, really and truly happy at dreaming and finding things good, and because you find some of them good, feeling good yourself.' " Then in an extraordinary passage, Larsen turns his observations upon himself and admits that he finds himself wishing at times that he was " 'blind to the facts of life and only knew its fancies

[4]The symbolism involved in Larsen's headaches has not been understood by critics. Charles Walcutt writes that Larsen "is destroyed by an unknown and adventitious something within him that could hardly be shown to represent society's hostility to his kind" (*American Literary Naturalism*, pp. 112-113).

Matthew J. Bruccoli writes that "as an attack on anti-social individualism *The Sea Wolf* is clearly open to criticism on the ground that Larsen is not finally defeated by social forces, or even by a particular antagonist, but a mysterious ailment that has no connection with social doctrine" ("Introduction," *The Sea Wolf*, p. ix).

[5]Kenneth S. Lynn, *The Dream of Success* (Boston, 1955) views *The Sea Wolf* as "a double-barreled attack on American capitalism" and the story of "Wolf Larsen, the natural-born fighting aristocrat, whose tragedy is that he has never been allowed to rise to the position to which his abilities entitle him" (pp. 92-93). Because Larsen has been frustrated by external and environmental circumstances, Lynn says, he has turned inward upon himself, dissipating his energies in torturing his crew and "his ambition in endless brooding about what might have been" (p. 95). Lynn states: "Massive headaches are the primary symbol of his frustation—they have plagued him for years, and in the course of the action they become progressively more severe, reducing him at times to agonized helplessness" (p. 95). Lynn is in error in his dating the duration of Larsen's headaches. London writes in *The Sea Wolf*: " 'I've never been sick in my life, Hump,' [Larsen] said, as [Hump] guided him to his room. 'Nor did I ever have a headache except the time my head was healing after having been laid open for six inches by a capstan bar' " (p. 69).

and illusions.' " Further, he judges in favor of illusion: " 'I often doubt, I often doubt [he says] the worthwhileness of reason. Dreams must be more substantial and satisfying.' "

To Maud's suggestion that he enlarge his world-view so as to include these "fancies and illusions," Larsen answers (in Hump's words, "all regretfully"): " 'Too late: I'd like to, perhaps, but I can't. My pocketbook is stuffed with the old coinage, and it's a stubborn thing. I can never bring myself to recognize anything else as valid.' "[6]

Wolf Larsen's subsequent escape from his brother Death Larsen, however, reassures him in his materialism and creates in him the illusion of his own personal triumph over Death itself. Under the sway of this illusion, he preaches Lucifer's "passion of revolt" to Hump and Maud. In his sexual attack upon Maud, Larsen then attempts to refute the idealism of Hump and Maud and to assert the primacy of materialism. Yet this refutation is not so easily effected, for unbeknown to Wolf Larsen (and this I take to be the central conflict embodying the theme of the novel), Wolf Larsen is animal-man in the process of becoming human.[7] The consequence, therefore, of

[6]Maud and Hump are not the only idealists on board the *Ghost*. The sailor Johnson (who, it will be remembered, signed for his cruise because of the *beauty* of the *Ghost*) serves as a reminder to Hump of the truth of idealism. Hump says of Johnson's defiance of Larsen: "And in his action I found complete refutation of all Wolf Larsen's materialism. The sailor Johnson was swayed by idea, by principle, and truth, and sincerity. He was right, he knew he was right, and he was unafraid. He would die for the right if needs be, he would be true to himself, sincere with his soul. And in this was portrayed the victory of the spirit over the flesh, the indomitability and moral grandeur of the soul that knows no restriction and rises above time and space and matter with a surety and invincibleness born of nothing else than eternity and immortality" (pp. 79-80).

That this pointing towards the efficacy of idealism was conscious on London's part is indicated by the "Textual Note" of Matthew J. Bruccoli (*The Sea Wolf*, pp. 1-2). Bruccoli reveals that "three important passages were added after serialization by London." Two of these three passages (all three are in Chapter XII) have to do with Hump's admiration for and Larsen's derision of Johnson's moral position. The third counterpoints the first two by portraying Hump after both Johnson's and Mugridge's beatings as realizing that the brutality of his environment has begun to coarsen him and that he is in danger of losing his own soul.

[7]Jack London returned to the theme of animal-man in the process of becoming human in *Before Adam* (1906) and *Martin Eden* (1909). *Before Adam* (New York, 1911), London's story of a boy's racial memories, describes the evolution of primitive beings, "half man, and half ape, and yet not ape, and not yet man." The boy hero (Big-Tooth) describes his arch enemy (Red-Eye) and comments upon his place in the "horde's" community: "Red-Eye was an atavism. He was the great discordant element in our horde. He was more primitive than any of us.He did not belong with us, yet we were still so primitive ourselves that we were incapable of a cooperative effort strong enough to cast him out. Rude as was our social organization, he was, nevertheless, too rude to live in it. He tended always to destroy the horde by his unsocial acts. *He was really a reversion to an earlier type, and his place was with the Tree People rather than with us who were in the process of becoming human*" (italics mine) (p. 111).

This same theme is sounded again in *Martin Eden* (New York, 1957). Before his disillusionment with the cultured Morses, Martin Eden sees himself as a brute-man in the process of becoming etheralized. Eden says: "Saints in heaven—how could they be anything but fair and pure? No praise to them. But saints in slime—ah, that was the everlasting wonder! That was what made life worthwhile. *To see moral grandeur rising out of the cesspools of iniquity; to rise himself and first glimpse beauty, faint and far, through mud-dripping eyes; to see out of weakness, and frailty, and viciousness, and all abysmal brutishness, arising strength, and truth, and high spiritual endowment*" (italics mine) (p. 115).

his attack upon Maud is not the proving the triumph of materialism but rather the furthering the destruction of his own animal self. For as a result of Larsen's attack upon Maud, he suffers another of his headaches, and this time the headache ends in his blindness.[8]

That Wolf Larsen has indeed been fragmented by the incursion of idealism can be seen in what happens after the *Ghost* drifts onto Endeavor Island. Larsen, understanding that Hump intends to usurp his command and to repair the *Ghost*, says to Hump: " 'It seems as though you're standing on your own legs at last, Hump' " and " 'I see you're working my philosophy back on me for all it is worth. But don't make the mistake of underestimating me. For your own good I warn you.' "

What should be emphasized here is twofold: first, that the education that Larsen had promised Hump when he came on board the *Ghost* is now complete (Hump is now standing on his own legs) and second, that Larsen gives Hump a warning to beware of him for his own good. This warning, as Hump quickly points out, is inconsistent with Larsen's philosophy of self-interest and is indicative that a change has been wrought in Larsen by his contact with the two idealistic lovers.

Yet even though Larsen warns Hump, he must at the same time attempt to kill him, not from any desire to keep Hump from repairing the *Ghost*, but so that he can give the lie to the failure of materialism. Queried by Hump as to why he had tried to kill him, Larsen says: " 'Oh, just to be alive, to be living and doing, to be the biggest bit of the ferment to the end, to eat you. But to die this way—' " Like the Lucifer he is often compared to, Wolf Larsen, who has lost his old harmony with a materialistic world, can assuage his anguish only by the act of destroying. But Larsen, unlike Lucifer,

[8]There is at first reading what may seem a problem involved in dating the onset of Larsen's blindness. After Larsen's abortive attack upon Maud, he covers his eyes and, calling for Hump, tells him that he is a sick man and asks him to help him to his bunk. Hump and Maud then desert the ship and next encounter Larsen after the *Ghost* has drifted ashore on Endeavor Island. Hump stumbles upon Larsen on board the ship and immediately notices "that his eyes were strange, not only the expression, but the physical seeming, as though the optic nerves and supporting muscles had suffered strain and slightly twisted the eyeballs." At this time Hump cocks both barrels of his shotgun, steps to the corner of the cabin, and then, after being challenged by Larsen, to shoot, clears his throat. Immediately after Hump has cleared his throat, Larsen addresses him by name. The fact of Larsen's addressing Hump could suggest that Larsen at this time still has the power of sight and only goes blind in the interval between his first and second encounter with Hump. It is more likely, however, that Larsen is blind and judges that it is Hump who is before him from the sound of Hump's feet on the deck, Hump's failure to fire the shotgun after having cocked it, and the sound of Hump's clearing his throat. The second explanation is more satisfactory because it explains 1) why Wolf Larsen must ask Hump the bearings of the island and 2) why, when Hump (who is surprised at Larsen's question) asks what were Larsen's last observations, Larsen smiles "inscrutably" and does not answer. Further this second explanation clarifies Larsen's reply when Hump asks what Larsen was doing when he was boarded by Death Larsen and his crew deserted him: " 'My best, you may be sure, which wasn't much under the circumstances.' "

is flesh and blood with his antagonists, his Edenic lovers, and as such cannot (as could Lucifer) consecrate himself to their destruction.

The final effect of Hump's and Maud's idealism upon Larsen, then, is manifested in the destruction of Larsen's magnificent animal strength. That this is so is evidenced by the circumstances involved in Larsen's last two attacks—the first leaving him blind, the second paralyzed. Both of these attacks occur propitiously just in time to save first Maud and later Hump from Larsen's animal brutality and assertion of the triumph of materialism. This saving of both Maud and Hump by Larsen's two separate attacks is London's method of revealing symbolically the inability of Larsen to destroy the two people who have instructed him in idealism and who represent that idealistic aspect of himself that is being born within him even as his animal self is being destroyed. With his second attack, Larsen becomes paralyzed and loses *the power of motion* that heretofore had signified for him the meaning of life.[9]

One might question, moreover, whether at his death Larsen still believes in materialism or whether he himself has not lost his faith. For just shortly before he dies (after Hump has resuscitated him from death by suffocation, an act which symbolically parallels Larsen's resuscitation of Hump), Larsen scrawls a message. "...I am all here, Hump....I can think more clearly than ever in my life before." This late statement of Larsen's, employing as it does the motif of inner vision, compares and contrasts with his earlier statement to Hump when the *Ghost* was under the trade winds. Larsen has said: " 'I know truth, divine good from evil, right from wrong. My vision is clear and far. I could almost believe in God.' " In the earlier passage when Wolf Larsen was in full command of his powers and when he believed that the meaning of life was motion, his world was limited to an outer vision. And yet under the influence of *beauty* (throughout the novel a corollary of idealism), Larsen felt intimation of God. But in the second and later passage, Larsen lies blind and paralyzed, incapable of either sight or motion. Nevertheless, Larsen finds that now, blind and paralyzed though he is, he can think more clearly than ever before. What London suggests is that as a result of Wolf Larsen's being raised from death, he has experienced illumination, an illumination perceived through an inner rather than an outer vision, and whose truth is idealism rather than materialism.[10]

[9]See my earlier citation (*Sea Wolf*, p. 76) on Larsen and life as the power of movement.

[10]My contention that Larsen's illumination arises from his inner vision and as a concomitant of his loss of animal power has a parallel in London's later (1915) novel of racial memory and transmigration, *The Star Rover*. In this novel, London gives to his protagonist (Darrell Standing) the power to will the death of his body and thus to release his soul to wander amid the stars, reliving its previous incarnations. Standing's power to accomplish this release of the soul

Larsen's last word, "B-O-S-H," is his refusal, however, to admit to Maud and Hump any intimation of immortality. Hump comments that Larsen remains "sceptical and invincible" to the end. As such Larsen remains true to his materialistic allegiance and in so doing gathers about him the trappings of a fatalistic and doomed hero. Finally, Wolf Larsen dramatizes and makes tragic the theme of animal-man in the process of becoming human, torn between his old natural harmony with a materialistic world and his attraction to a new and idealistic world. It is not then as naturalistic superman that Wolf Larsen is meaningful, but as man in conflict, torn between allegiance to his animal reason or acquiesence to his human heart.

is dependent, however, upon his body being physically weakened and bound immobile in a strait jacket. The result of his "star roving" is that Standing, who entered prison a scientist dedicated to material fact and objective reality, comes to believe that his impending death by hanging is only the State's puny effort to destroy him. He now knows the essence of man is his spirit and his spirit is immortal.

The Transformation of Material in a Mimetic Fiction

GORDON MILLS

London's use of experiences from his own life in his fiction has been discussed often. The important consideration, however, should not be the propriety of using such material, but rather the success of the work as a whole. London's use of his own experiences in Martin Eden *provides a basis for Professor Mills' investigation of this subject. The primary criterion for judging the effectiveness of the transformation of such material lies in its ability to create illusion.* Martin Eden *contains both successful and unsuccessful transformations of material from London's own experience. The successful ones have been selected and controlled by London so that they become a part of the believable actions of the characters in the novel. The unsuccessful ones suffer from an excess of sentimentality and from problems in point of view.*

Probably everyone would concede that all of Jack London's full-length novels and most of his short stories are, as works of art, demonstrably and seriously flawed in one way or another. Why, then, do many sophisticated readers continue to find his work appealing, as they unquestionably do?

At worst, we might seem to confront the kind of merely psychological puzzle René Wellek had in mind when he remarked about Chernyshevsky's *What Is To Be Done?*, "This incredibly bad novel altered . . . the whole direction of the lives of important men."[1] *Martin Eden's* comparable effectiveness in inspiring people to great effort has often been remarked upon.[2] So far as I know, however, *Martin Eden* has never been described as an incredibly bad novel; our problem in

[1]*Concepts of Criticism* (New Haven, CT: Yale University Press, 1963), p. 245.

[2]See Franklin Walker, "Martin Eden," *The American Novel: From James Fenimore Cooper to William Faulkner*, ed. Wallace Stegner (New York: Basic Books, 1965), p. 134.

trying to understand its appeal is by no means limited to peculiarities in the emotional life of readers who enjoy it. On the other hand, in accepting as fact the power of London's fiction despite its weaknesses, we are forced to ponder our concept of either art or literary sophistication, or both. We begin to understand what Wolfgang Iser had in mind when he recently pointed out the need for a theory of literary effect.[3] Although in the following discussion I will not be particularly observant of Iser's phenomenological methods and I will certainly not be attempting to articulate a theory of literary effect, I will try to discuss both the weaknesses and the strengths of London's fiction in ways which will throw some light on how that fiction acts upon its readers. For this purpose, I will limit my discussion to *Martin Eden,* London's own favorite among his novels.

There is general agreement as to the primary weaknesses in London's fiction: the language is often mawkish;[4] ideas are not always effectively integrated with other elements of a work;[5] in his full-length novels London has trouble with structure and point of view; there is an embarrassing amount of self-dramatizing by the author;[6] and drama tends to collapse into sentimentality.[7] In London's best work, chiefly his stories of the North, these faults are either absent or inconspicuous. But, of course, freedom from such faults is by itself no assurance of greatness; there seems little disposition to claim for London a place among what Clifton Fadiman used to call the major authors.[8] Our problem is to discern by what means, given his limitations, London nevertheless worked such magic as to evoke, two generations after his death, the kind of interest represented by this issue of *Modern Fiction Studies.*

The source of emotional power in any mimetic fiction must lie principally in its illusional quality. Hegel, and Susanne Langer,

[3]*The Implied Reader* (Baltimore, MD: Johns Hopkins University Press, 1974), p. xii. Subsequent references cited in text.

[4]Irving Stone suggests that the mawkish language in which the love affair in *The Sea-Wolf* is presented resulted from London's exposure to the sentimental letters, often thousands of words long, Charmian Kittredge wrote to him before their marriage. This style, persisting into the love story in *Martin Eden,* is certainly unlike the crisp language of the Northland stories or of the description of action in *Martin Eden.* See *Sailor on Horseback* (New York: Houghton Mifflin, 1938), p. 207. Subsequent references cited in text.

[5]E.g. Franklin Walker, "Ideas and Action in Jack London's Fiction," *Essays on American Literature in Honor of Jay Hubbell,* ed. Clarence Gohdes (Durham, NC: Duke University Press, 1967), pp. 259-272.

[6]E.g. Sam S. Baskett, "Introduction," in Jack London, *Martin Eden,* Rinehart Edition (New York: Rinehart and Company, 1956), pp. xiv-xv, xvi-xvii. Subsequent references cited in text.

[7]E.g. Earle Labor, *Jack London* (New York: Twayne Publishers, 1974), p. 148. Subsequent references cited in text.

[8]E.g. Labor, in the "Preface" to *London,* identifies him as a "major figure" in American literature and surely this designation is appropriate.

would prefer the word "semblance" to "illusion" and would mean something a little more than the word *illusion* can comfortably accommodate; but illusion will serve our purpose, which is limited to consideration of a mimetic work. An illusion is an experience of the imagination. It is a fiction. The illusion created by mimetic literature requires setting, coherence, wholeness. The setting assures the observer that what he will see is an illusion, not a decision-demanding reality. Observing a make-believe riot within the setting of the stage of a theater or within the covers of a novel is a very different experience from actually being in a riot. The setting signifies illusion, but it does not indicate much about the particular character of the illusion to be experienced. That particularity emerges from the wholeness and coherence the reader or observer senses in the work. Halfway through a reading of Beckett's *Molloy* no reader could continue with an unimpaired illusion were he to discover some pages from *Paradise Lost* interpolated into the text. In Jean Piaget's terms, we are concerned with *wholeness, transformation,* and *genesis.*

Wholeness, in a complex entity, implies an internal relational principle. The parts of the whole are bound together in some way in which they are not bound to the external environment. The whole is a totality made up of related parts, and one totality can be distinguished from another.

The ideas of transformation and genesis are concerned with the creation of a totality, in the sense just indicated. I will comment on the idea of transformation, delaying the idea of genesis until a little later. A whole, or totality, is created through transformation. In the context of Piaget's psychology, one totality, or psychological structure, is created by the transformation of another psychological structure, or structures. An example is the emergence of a child's ability, at the age of seven or eight, to grasp the principle of the conservation of matter. The emergence of this psychological structure in the child's mind requires the transformation of other structures which had already been present. Comparably, the creation of a work of fiction, regarded as a totality, depends on the transformation of materials the author takes from the world around him. These materials, or structures, are transformed into the illusional quality of art. Whether we should think of this process as the transformation of a group of structures into another structure, as Piaget does in his psychological studies, is of little importance. For our purposes, Hegel's—and Langer's—word "material" will do as well as "structure" to designate what is transformed and will prove to be more convenient. This would not be true, however, if we were seeking a completely rigorous articulation of the process from Piaget's point of view.

Martin Eden is a mimetic fiction, and our subject now becomes the problem of how materials are transformed into the parts of the illusion constituted by a mimetic fiction considered as a totality or structure. A simple analogy to another representational art, landscape painting, indicates the answer. Consider a landscape painting reproduced in the form of a jigsaw puzzle which has been completely assembled except for one last piece. The one remaining piece, it happens, is colored a uniform blue. It is a "material"; it is only a piece of blue cardboard. Yet the moment this piece is inserted into its proper place in the assembled jigsaw puzzle, the blue cardboard is transformed into blue sky. The way in which we perceive the piece of blue cardboard has been transformed by its relationship to the totality of the illusion in which it appears.

Of course, we now have a paradox on our hands. The illusion as a totality is created through transformation of the parts, but the parts are transformed only by their relationship to the totality. Since it is an unmistakable fact that materials are transformed into parts of illusions, we need not pursue this paradox for our consideration of *Martin Eden.* My own opinion is that the paradox is resolved through the concept of the artist's controlling purpose, his initial grasp of his work as a totality. This opinion, however, is incipiently at odds with Piaget's concept of genesis. Genesis, Piaget says, is a system of transformations leading from one state to another more stable state.[9] *Genesis* is a narrower term than *transformation.* Any change of one structure into another is a transformation, but genesis is a change, a transformation, only from a given structure to a more stable structure. In this idea there might appear to be a reinforcement of the solution I myself suggested for the paradox, but it is appearance only. As may be seen in the current state of structuralist poetics, a problem associated with such a concept as genesis, when applied to literature, is a tendency to displace the role of the imagination of the author with a mere process. This problem may well establish a limit beyond which structuralist poetics cannot pass; nevertheless, for our present objective we can employ the eminently useful concepts of wholeness and transformation without concern for these remoter theoretical issues or the paradox which lies within them.

One of the materials London incorporated into *Martin Eden* was himself. "I was Martin Eden," he wrote, defending himself against the charge that Martin Eden could not possibly have achieved so great a success so rapidly.[10] The nature of their great energy and

[9]*Six Psychological Studies* (New York: Vintage Books, 1968), p. 144. For a further discussion of terminology, see the first chapter of Piaget's *Structuralism,* tr. Chaninah Maschler (New York: Harper and Row, 1970).

[10]In *John Barleycorn* (New York: Century Company, 1913), p. 242.

the chronology of their success are indeed much the same for the author and his fictional character, as is the chronology of their subsequent despair. Like Martin Eden, London asserts that when he had achieved success he discovered he despised it. "Success" was his first choice of a title for the novel, "Star-Dust" his second, "Martin Eden" only his third. Like Martin Eden, London declared himself appalled by the men and women he found inhabiting the social world he had sought so eagerly to enter. But, unlike Martin Eden, London—in *John Barleycorn*—described himself as having been rescued from despair and restored to happiness. The agent of his restoration, he says, was his faith in "the people"—a faith he finally dismissed as a fantasy. It was of course lack of such a faith to which London attributes Martin's destruction. The validity of London's own restoration is open to question.

By 1909, when *Martin Eden* appeared, London was one of the most famous people in the world. It was no secret that this novel was in many ways autobiographical. In pondering the effectiveness of the work, we therefore seem to be at once confronted with the question of whether its appeal lies in its autobiographical factuality or in its illusional power as a work of art. Reasonable though it appears, however, this question is somewhat misleading. Illusional power is no stranger to the pages of either history or autobiography. Surely everyone would agree that long stretches of the historical works of Francis Parkman or Arthur M. Schlesinger, Jr., move with the intensity of fiction. In *Life in the Far West* George F. Ruxton presented his personal experience with the mountain men as a novel. P. J. Bouman modeled his historical work *Revolution of the Lonely* on the fictional technique of John Dos Passos. And now we have the nonfiction novel and Gonzo journalism. As Macaulay in his essay "History" said long ago, history "is sometimes fiction; it is sometimes theory . . . history begins in novel and ends in essay."[11] Our problem in *Martin Eden* is not factuality but what was done with factuality; it is not whether readers see glimpses of the real Jack London in the story but what is done with the real Jack London they see.

From this point of view it becomes apparent that the presence of the real Jack London in the story sometimes lends power to the illusion but at other times constitutes a flaw. The author was not uniformly successful in the transformation of the material constituted by his own experience.

Let us consider first one of the successful transformations. For this purpose, no part of the novel is more interesting than that initial

[11]For a recent discussion of Macaulay's place in historiography see Ihor Sevčenko, "Two Varieties of Historical Writing," *History and Theory*, 8 (1969), 332-345.

section in which Martin first becomes aware of the world of the Morses and strives to make himself worthy of it. The dominant movement of this section, its wholeness, can be initially formulated as the relationship between the two concepts of vitality and a transcendent reality. Out of the vital force embodied in Martin Eden emerges a vision of a transcendent reality, initiated by his sudden introduction to the Morses; the early part of the novel is a depiction of the movement of this vital force in the direction established by the vision. The entire process can be understood as a transformation of the material of London's personal experience. At its simplest this transformation is only an idealizing, a romanticizing, but in the end it is much more complex than that.

So far as mere animal vitality is concerned, little transformation appears to have been needed. Tributes to London's own superabundant spirits and contagious enthusiasm are found everywhere. His friend Anna Strunsky, for example, wrote of him, "To know him was immediately to receive an accelerated enthusiasm about everybody" (Stone, p. 125). It is only a short step to London's comment that for Martin Eden "life was so strange and wonderful" (*Martin Eden,* p. 108). In the novel, London's need was simply to give this vitality its necessary direction toward the love and beauty contained in his vision rather than toward, or not only toward, the mere acquisition of wealth. In actuality, London's feelings were evidently mixed. He contributed his time and effort freely to the cause of socialism, for instance, but meanwhile asserted his willingness to sell himself outright to the magazines (Stone, p. 160). Martin Eden, on the other hand, regarded wealth as an inadquate motive for undergoing severe privation as an apprentice, in contrast to the motive of "the love of a woman, or... attainment of beauty" (*Martin Eden,* p. 68). Throughout the early portion of the novel, Martin's intense aspirations are controlled principally by the idealism of his vision. In addition to a superabundance of enthusiasm, a second element is present in Martin's vitality, one leading into complexities to which we must return later. This is the element of the natural world, the forcefulness of nature itself, of which Martin partakes. He is, in effect, borne into the story on a sea wind, under a brilliant sky. He has that "natural" vitality which the primitivistic Robert Beverley, writing in 1705, associated with Indians, as in Beverley's comment that among Indian girls "the excess of Life and Fire, which they never fail to have, makes them frolicksome...."[12]

A full apprehension of the transformation of London's vitality

[12]Quoted in Leo Marx, *The Machine in the Garden* (New York: Oxford University Press, 1967), p. 80.

into that of Martin Eden cannot be separated from the vision associated with that vitality. Martin's vision of a world of love, beauty, and intellectuality was of course false, and a particularly interesting question is the degree to which London had ever himself experienced such a vision. The power of the novel is heavily dependent on the great gap between the seaman's world of Martin Eden and the gentility of the Morse home on which Martin centers his vision. Had London himself ever undergone the full impact of an encounter involving so great a disparity as that between Martin Eden and the Morses? The possibility that in principle such encounters may indeed occur is poignantly demonstrated in a comment by Eldridge Cleaver, written while he was in prison:

> Through reading I was amazed to discover how confused people were. I had thought that, out there beyond the horizon of my own ignorance, unanimity existed, that even though I myself didn't know what was happening in the universe other people certainly did.[13]

Pondering such a statement, we see that to create as intense as possible an illusion of enthrallment by a vision of love, beauty, and intellectuality, London faced a very concrete problem. He had to establish the greatest conceivable distance between the actual circumstances of his protagonist and the supposed embodiment of his protagonists's vision. Given enough distance, the fact that the real Morse household was by no means isomorphic with his vision could go unnoticed by the protagonist. Anything which unnecessarily lessened the gap between Martin's own situation and what he mistakenly believed to be the situation in the Morse home had to be rejected as unsuitable material. Were London to have allowed Martin the status of a student in the University of California when he first entered the Morse home, for instance, the illusion sought would have vanished, or at best would have lost much of its intensity. In fact, Jack London was a student at the University of California within months of his first visit to the real-life original of the Morse home and was, unlike Martin Eden, at the age of nineteen enrolled in the Oakland High School when this first visit was made. It was through his membership in the Henry Clay Debating Society, a club for people with intellectual interests, that London became acquainted with Edward Applegarth, who took him home and introduced him to his sister Mabel, on whom Ruth Morse was modeled.

These facts from London's personal experience were not suitable material; they would have brought Martin Eden much too close to

[13] *Soul on Ice* (New York: Dell Publishing Co., 1968), p. 5.

the Morse life-style. Their transformation would have required a quite different totality. On the other hand, many of the events of London's past were indeed readily adaptable: his life at sea; his decision, while a hobo, to acquire an education; the nature of his relationship with Mabel Applegarth; his prodigious efforts to learn to write. It should be remembered, however, that although these events may have a certain interest in themselves, it is only when they are integrated into the "wholeness" of *Martin Eden* that they take on the intensity of art.

Yet it is generally agreed that London was by no means uniformly successful in transforming his personal experience into the illusional quality of art. The meaning of transformation is, in fact, clarified by examination of an instance or two of failure. We might begin by considering one of the mirror scenes. Martin repeatedly talks to his image in a mirror (*Martin Eden,* pp. 31, 96, 101, 107, 120, 128). His first such talk is very brief, but is preceded by a long and thoughtful examination of his reflected appearance. Possibly the face he sees in the mirror is not that of Jack London; the trouble is, if it is not London's face, there is no way to prove it is not and every reason to suspect that it is. The features described bear a remarkable resemblance to photographs of London: high forehead, mop of brown hair, blue eyes, square chin.

> Above a square-domed forehead he [Martin Eden] saw a mop of brown hair, nut-brown, with a wave to it and hints of curls that were a delight to any woman, making hands tingle to stroke it, and fingers tingle to pass caresses through it.... He wondered if there was soul in those steel-gray eyes that were often quite blue of color and that were strong with the briny airs of the sun-washed deep.... His might have been a cherub's mouth.... The chin and jaw, strong and just hinting of square aggressiveness.... (pp. 31-32)

There are three separate difficulties here. The first is the absurd romanticizing or idealizing ("cherub's mouth"). The second is the ambiguity of the point of view. We are seeing through Martin Eden's eyes ("he saw...he wondered"), but what we are seeing becomes quite embarrassing if we regard it as Martin's stream of consciousness. Consequently, we nervously jump back and forth from Martin's point of view to the omniscient author's point of view, and neither seems right. The third difficulty is the problem of transformation. We helplessly associate the description of Martin's appearance with that of London himself and then wonder what Jack London's personal appearance has to do with the story. The intensity of the illusion is surely diminished as we face this somehow irritating practical question.

This third difficulty does not arise from our association of the author with Martin Eden. Quite the contrary: our glimpses of the real Jack London through the veil of fiction often heighten the intensity of the illusional quality of the novel. Knowing that the plausibility of the illusion we are absorbed in is derived from events in real life, we abandon ourselves to it; we grant our assent, even while mindful that the story has the transformed wholeness of art rather than the raggedness of life. An instance of this kind of response to another work is seen in the report of Houghton Mifflin's reader concerning London's first collection of short stories:

> He draws a vivid picture of the terrors of cold, darkness, and starvation, the pleasures of human companionship in adverse circumstances, and the sterling qualities which the rough battle with nature brings out. *The reader is convinced that the author has lived the life himself.* (Stone, p. 123, italics mine)

The difficulty is not that Martin Eden is Jack London but that it is so hard to avoid regarding Martin's absorbed contemplation of his image in the mirror as a narcissistic compulsion of the author's ego. Had the structural wholeness of the illusion the novel creates required that the features described resemble London's features, as the structural wholeness clearly requires that the intensity of Martin's efforts to learn to write resemble London's own efforts, there would have been no transformational problem. The illusion would have been unimpaired. Unfortunately, no such requirement is evident as far as Martin's personal appearance is concerned, and the reader is forced into an unpleasant choice he would much rather not have to make. Is he witnessing an emotionally effective element in the esthetic illusion of Martin Eden's movement toward his vision, one in which Martin first truly confronts the question, "Who am I?"—or is he witnessing a compulsive narcissistic ritual on the part of Jack London? Of course, the reader should never have been presented with such a dilemma.

A fundamental principle seems to be involved. A writer can make use of his personal experience so long as that experience is unquestionably subordinate to the totality of the illusion. It is when a reader unavoidably begins to feel that an author's intrusion of himself into the story is directly self-serving in some way, a begging for sympathy or for admiration, that the illusion is damaged. A rather obvious intrusion may go virtually unnoticed if it seems to be entirely subservient to an appropriate structural totality, as with the obvious presence of London himself in the learning-to-write scenes. To feel ourselves in the presence of a truly great literary work, we must at no time doubt that the author is thinking of the illusion he is creating as a means of exploring human experience rather than as a direct outlet for his personal emotions. The writer must evidently perceive himself only as one of the materials to be transformed into an esthetic illusion if he is to make effective use of his own feelings in the process.

A second instance of a failure of transformation might be taken from the episode in Chapter Fifteen of Martin's reverie about his fight, years before, with Cheese-Face. This is a surprisingly long section, around three thousand words, in which Martin lives again in his imagination a series of fights he had with Cheese-Face, beginning when he was six and Cheese-Face eight and terminating when Martin was seventeen. The last fight, which is described in detail, is a melodramatic set-piece. It takes place at night, each fighter backed by a gang. After the fight has been going on for some time without advantage to either side, Cheese-Face sneakily hits Martin with brass knuckles, causing "ghastly damage." Martin's gang starts to rush in, but Martin wants the fight to continue and warns them back: "They shrank away from him. They were brutes, but he was the arch-brute, a thing of terror that towered over them and dominated them" (p. 126). Later Martin's right arm is broken, but he fights on with only his left arm and wins.

The spirit of this episode is reminiscent of F. Scott Fitzgerald's report that for years he put himself to sleep at night by a fantasy in which, with bandaged head, he made a goal-line stand in the closing moments of a football game. Martin Eden arises from his own reverie to address the mirror: " 'A bit of hysteria and melodrama, eh?' he queried" (p. 128).

As a melodramatic fantasy through which the reader is made aware that Martin is being overstrained by too much work, too little sleep, and too little encouragement from Ruth, the episode could be tremendously effective. Unfortunately, it is presented as a memory of actual events rather than an escape into fantasy. Only at the end does a possible hint come in the words "hysteria and melodrama," and even then these words may refer not to the events themselves but to Martin's indulging himself in reminiscence.

In this second instance of failure, the material which resists transformation is not the author's self but rather actions which simply cannot be contained by the totality with which London was working. It is not inconceivable that, like Martin, a six-year-old boy would voluntarily day after day take a brutal beating from an eight-year-old boy; or that in the later fight, when he was seventeen, Martin would go on to win after receiving a ghastly wound from brass knuckles and having his right arm broken. The problem is that we have not been sufficiently prepared to accept these incidents as natural although astonishing elements within the totality through which we are moving. As a unit, the Cheese-Face episode is well conceived: it serves to counterpoint the immediately preceding chapter in which Ruth had told Martin his writing was degrading; it established her utter inability to grasp the significance of his personal experience of life and the objectives of his writing. And possibly the fact that Martin indulges in this reverie at all is intended to reveal an almost intolerable physical and emotional strain. But instead of serving these purposes with undivided effect, the particulars within the unit intractably call attention to their own melodramatic character. What sort of totality would be necessary to contain them? Perhaps—to take one instance only—the behavior of the six-year-old Martin, and of his antagonist Cheese-Face as well, could be successfully handled in a slow-moving, thoughtful psychological study. In any case, granted that the events in the Cheese-Face episode are not inconceivable, that they might even be historical facts, they have not been, in Iser's way of putting it, made probable by fiction (Iser, p. 92).

Before we turn back to further consideration of sources of power in the book, we should take a moment for one instance of what may at first seem to be a difficulty in transformation but which actually is not. Let us consider the role of abstract ideas in the story: essentially, human brotherhood versus unbridled individualism, or Marx versus Nietzsche, with all the paraphernalia of turn-of-the-century ideas carried in their wake. At first glance it may seem that these abstractions come too directly from London himself, without sufficient transformation through internalization in the experience of the chatacters, but this notion is not easy to support. The fact is, the part played in this novel by most of the ideas associated with it is trivial. I should emphasize that I refer not to the innate importance of such ideas as Marxism and individualism or to the interest of London's treatment of them but to their function within the story. Everyone agrees that socialism is given inadequate treatment. And although Martin makes a good many comments about the ideas of Spencer and Nietzsche, the content of these ideas has virtually no effect on the course of his life—with the single exception that he never plays the part of a worker for socialism. The role of these ideas is actually to embody the excitement of intellectuality itself, and in this limited role their transformation is effective. Advocate of individualism though he may be, Martin is operationally a socialist, in the terms in which London understood socialism, which meant a sort of secular Christian brotherhood. Martin is, on the whole, tolerant of others; he is carelessly generous with his money; he is never snobbish. A poignant moment occurs when, out with Ruth for the first time, Martin sees Lizzie Connolly and lifts his hat to her: "He could not be disloyal to his kind." The course of Martin's life is not a problem in ideology.

Although the source of power in *Martin Eden* does not lie in those philosophical ideas ostensibly involved in the novel, it nevertheless is linked to an idea, but an idea which is so pervasive a part of American life that it is more orientation than concept. Fundamentally, this idea or orientation is pastoralism, which for our purposes can be defined simply as a desire for a harmonious fusion of the "natural" and the cultured. As others have noted, Martin comes out of the sea to a direct encounter with that most exotic of the symbols of culture, a Victorian maiden. Given this pastoral model, a refinement of our initial version of the dominant movement in the first section, we can discern the essential form of the illusion London created and the effectiveness of the transformations involved.

Most abstractly, *Martin Eden* is an articulation of the proposition that when the symbol systems of a high culture become too remote from those direct perceptions out of which they were derived, the systems degenerate. Martin's way of phrasing this proposition is his assertion that Professor Caldwell lacks biology. In a recent article the distinguished physicist Eugene Wigner expresses, in principle, the same fundamental proposition in terms more familiar to our own time when he says that physics can never become a complete, self-contained symbol system because of its ultimate dependence on "primitive observations."[14] Needless to say, the function of such an idea as this in *Martin Eden* is not trivial.

The pastoral model of course translates this proposition into psychological terms. Let us turn to anthropologist Kenelm Burridge's book *Encountering Aborigines* for a formulation. Discussing the opposition between "rational objectivity" and what he calls "participation in oneness"—or what Martin Eden calls "sublime carelessness"—Burridge makes the comment quoted below; he might almost have been thinking of Martin's first interrogation of his mirror:

> When man first crossed the threshold and became aware of himself, he cut himself off from the natural world about him. Becoming morally responsible, obligated, man could no longer be like anything else in the world. But the impulse and desire to close the gap... to act in accordance only with the programmed instincts of nature, remains in all men.[15]

What *Martin Eden* affords the reader is the illusion of acting out this experience in the particularity of Martin's own circumstances. The

[14] "Epistemology of Quantum Mechanics—Its Appraisal and Demands," *Psychological Issues* VI, No. 2, Monograph 22, p. 27.

[15] (Elmsford, NY: Pergamon Press, 1973), p. 10.

circumstances are Martin's; the materials out of which they were created were London's. The wholeness of the illusion London creates and the significance of that structure in our own lives lend their force to the necessary transformations.

There is, nevertheless, an ambiguity in referring to the wholeness of an illusion which is marred by such failures of transformation as were observed earlier. It would seem, it must in fact be, impossible for any mature and thoughtful reader to escape occasionally being jarred out of his absorption in the story. On formalistic grounds we must give *Martin Eden* some low marks. We are forced into ambiguity, however, by the disparity between this novel's failure to meet formalistic demands and its demonstrated power to grip the attention of sophisticated readers. Logic seems to demand postulation of a wholeness which is more than the sum of the individual transformations contained in the work, although how this wholeness could be articulated is at present beyond the resources of literary theory. Psychoanalytic theory offers one attractive possibility, but the essentially static character of psychoanalytic interpretations has not yet been shown capable of responding effectively to the requirements of those dynamics of the reader-text relationship which can be observed daily by any thoughtful person. Roland Barthes, in his "codes," is working toward another kind of possibility, but is similarly faced with many unresolved problems.

No attempt to summarize a position with regard to the initial question of sophisticated readers' granting assent to a book like this one should be made without recognizing the paradoxical pessimism of the latter part of the story. Paradoxical, because Jack London's writing surges with vitality even in its depiction of Martin Eden's death-wish:

> He arose and thrust his head out of the port-hole, looking down into the milky wash. The *Mariposa* was deeply loaded, and, hanging by his hands, his feet would be in the water. He could slip in noiselessly. No one would hear. A smother of spray dashed up, wetting his face. It tasted salt on his lips, and the taste was good. He wondered if he ought to write a swan-song, but laughed the thought away. There was no time. He was too impatient to be gone.

The literal meaning of this latter part of the book points toward death, but the voice we hear is filled with life. From one perspective we can conclude only that in this paradox we see again a failure of transformation, a complaint about this part of the book which has, in other terms, been frequent (Baskett, p. xvi). Yet there is another possibility. Perhaps readers most often feel this book to be not so much a denial of life itself as a prophetic parable or as a questioning of the forms our life in the United States has taken. Looked at from this perspective, the latter part of *Martin Eden* particularizes the failurc of the pastoral dream. London embodies this experience in an attack on our culture. Have we done well? London says no.

Finally, then, it seems safe to say that a reader's experience with *Martin Eden* is in no sense a simple matter. Is *Martin Eden,* therefore, a book to which any sophisticated reader can give his assent? Remembering Wolfgang Iser's brilliant analysis of the dynamic relationship between a given reader's imagination and any given text, (Iser, pp. 274-294 *passim*), I can say only, "It depends." Yet we know that many sophisticated readers do testify to the affective quality of *Martin Eden* and do indicate their intellectual assent to its import–grimacing, meanwhile, over its flaws. And so in the end we seem forced to stand our initial proposition on its head and seek a more comprehensive literary theory than we yet possess. If the mere absence of flaws is no assurance of greatness, neither does the presence of serious flaws preclude enjoyment and the granting of intellectual assent. Clearly, what is wanted is indeed a theory of literary effect, a theory which will bring us closer to an understanding of that still mysterious experience exemplified in the statement of that man whose unsolicited letter Earle Labor quotes:

> I have for the past two evenings been absorbed completely (and I do mean *completely*) in *Martin Eden.* I am profoundly moved. Nothing else I have ever read has had this effect upon me.... (Labor, p. 116)

Jack London's *Martin Eden*: The Development of the Existential Hero

JONATHAN HAROLD SPINNER

Existential criticism is an over-used and often misunderstood approach to literature. However, this article provides some unique insights to the character of Martin Eden, and furthers the notion that London was a man ahead of his time in portraying the dilemma of modern man. The meaninglessness which Martin Eden faces is much like that described by later writers, that confrontation with nothingness which afflicts mid-twentieth century man. Martin Eden, finding the Horatio Alger myth of success to be false—that is, hard work does not necessarily bring success and happiness—discovers that he has become truly alienated from the modern world. His "work performed" is not enough to save him from death and destruction. Eden's alienation is made complete by his inability to return, after his success, to the lower class world which he left. Eden has gained knowledge and introspection, and has seen the absurdity of the natural world. He escapes, via suicide, and makes a final statement about the existential world.

Martin Eden is one of the first novels that documents the disintegration of the American success story, the final collapse of the Horatio Alger legend, the great fall of the Gospel of Wealth myth. Yet it also marks one of the first scenes in a new American drama, that of the existential dilemma of the modern anti-hero. If the book is seen only as a final chapter in the annals of the American success story, then it seems to be two separate, distinct, and unintegrated halves, with Martin Eden's behavior after becoming a successful novelist seemingly inexplicable. But by considering the novel as presenting some of the opening lines of the modern existential problem, *Martin Eden* becomes a complete and solid piece of work, and an enduring American novel.

Reprinted from *Michigan Academician,* III (Summer, 1970), pp. 43-48, by permission of the Michigan Academy of Science and Letters.

The Horatio Alger-Gospel of Wealth myth was the American statement to the world. The last quarter of the 19th century was imbued with it, the literature of the time is flooded with it. London's novel, written in the opening years of the 20th century appears, in its first chapters, to be yet another reflection of that guiding beacon of American thought. Martin Eden fully intends to succeed. The American dream of success is his dream of success. As he tells Ruth Morse, the "hackwork is only makeshift." Given two years, and he will make the editors sit up and take notice; they will be "glad" to buy his good work. For Eden has faith in himself. He knows, he says, "what I have in me."

So Eden, like any other young American, knows that through hard work, he will emerge victorious. Yet it is Eden's misfortune and folly, from the viewpoint of the traditional American dream, that he has chosen a course fraught with introspective perils, that of writing. Nor does Eden limit himself to magazine editing, or newspaper work; his ambition is fine writing and the rarified atmosphere of the mind. It is this attempt by Eden that leads him from the narrow, sure channels of the American dream to the broad, uncertain depths of the existential dilemma. One wonders if London realizes that Eden's introspectiveness is self-destructive. I doubt that he does, however, because of the parallelism in London's own life. As I intend to show, an unconscious thread of introspection as an avenue of death for those not strong enough to accept the discoveries that it presents, runs throughout the novel. But I believe it to be unconscious and unknown to London.

The modern existential dilemma, that overworked phrase, can be defined as the loss of identity, the feeling of alienation, the lack of faith so well-documented in so much of modern literature. A child of the industrial and scientific revolutions, one of its first propounders was Thomas Carlyle, in his book *Sartor Resartus.* This is one of the first modern works that carefully documents the loss of faith in an orderly universe because of the pressures of the industrial and scientific revolutions. Although the existential dilemma was hidden for three-quarters of a century in America behind the twin facades of the westering myth and the Horatio Alger legend, the myths of escape and success, *Martin Eden* breaks through as one of the first fictional statements of American existentialism.

Eden is the perfect name for an American Adamic hero who falls after eating of the Tree of Knowledge. If Eden is Adam, then his Eve is Ruth Morse, who bids him eat of the forbidden fruit of introspective self-awareness. Satan, if he does not whisper in Ruth's ear, speaks to her heart in more direct ways. Ruth sees Martin as a full-blooded, lower class, sexual Minotaur, with his "heavy corded, almost bull-like (neck), bronzed by the sun, spilling over with rugged health and strength." And although Ruth considers Eden's strength "gross and brutish," she is surely and steadily drawn to his phallic power. Freud would have been delighted.

It is ironic that the fragile, innocent Ruth Morse should tempt Eden, yet the apple she offers is, like Eve's, forbidden to Eden and so much desired. From his humble, lower-working class viewpoint, the bourgeois world-view is all encompassing and grand. Yet Eden does not accept Ruth's, or the middle class' view of obtaining wealth. From the first, he is intrigued by bourgeois education and knowledge, and not by the material goods that they possess. He intends to get that education and knowledge, for the middle class students in school with him, although physically his inferiors, could talk Ruth's "talk—the thought depressed him. But what was a brain for? . . . What they had done, he could do."

Thus far we have all the beginnings of an Horatio Alger story, a poor-boy-makes-good theme. Yet Eden has taken a fatal turn, for instead of turning outward toward the wealth and position of a Mr. Butler, he turns inward toward the bitter loss of faith of a Mr. Brissenden. We cannot carry the comparison of Brissenden and Eden too far, for Eden has been tempered in different fires, yet the comparison exists. Both are artists, both are disillusioned, and both are destroyed by the society and the intellectual climate that surrounds them. Both, as strong as they appear, are brittle, although both have been through much. Brissenden has been through sickness, through tuberculosus. Eden has been through Cheese Face and the laundry.

The Cheese Face and the laundry episodes are the most powerful in the novel. They have similar qualities, and are, indeed, extremely similar experiences. They are hard physical experiences, and Eden survives them both because of his endurance and ability to withstand physical pain. Yet as toughening as these experiences are, they do not prepare Eden for the mental toughness that the new industrial-scientific-existential age demands. It is interesting to note that Eden recalls the Cheese Face incident when he is at the bottom, when rejection slip after rejection slip has totally defeated him for the moment, when the Horatio Alger myth has been shattered, when long, hard work has brought no reward. It is then that he recalls his greatest triumph, it is then that he reminds himself that he can withstand any physical pain. After his reminiscent dream, he tells himself that he will succeed. However, there is a note of uncertainty in it, as though Eden realizes that this is a different battle he is in because as he tells himself, "You can't stop here. You've got to go on. It's to a finish, you know."

Similarly, the laundry is another test of Eden's physical endurance. Again his mind is overwhelmed by the physical, and as he fought like a brute against Cheese Face, so he works and lives like an animal in the laundry. As in the Cheese Face incident, Eden's mind, his introspective tool, is shattered. It is impossible for Eden to work like an animal and think on a high level at the same time. Physically, Eden is fairly well up to it, mentally he is destroyed by it. After three months of working at the laundry during the week, and bicycling to San Francisco to see Ruth on the weekends, Eden gets drunk with his partner Joe. "He forgot, and lived again, and living, he saw... the beast he was making of himself–not by the drink, but by the work." As he drunkenly realizes, it was not by being a "toil-beast" that he could succeed. This was the whiskey's message. "The whiskey was wise. It told secrets on itself."

Thus, on both occasions, it is work, hard work, that brings on a mental shattering in Eden. For Eden, Horatio Alger is proven wrong, hard work does not lead to success, but to death, a spiritual and intellectual one. These are premonitions of the stresses that Eden will soon face, they are indications of what Eden lacks, mental toughness. They are turning points in the book, because they both denote the destruction of the Horatio Alger myth, and the development of the existential dilemma that Eden is soon faced with. These two incidents are the links in the novel between the two opposite philosophical statements. If Eden cannot cope with Horatio Alger, how will he be able to cope with Jean Paul Sartre?

It is precisely because of Eden's introspection, the natural result of his profession, that the events of the second half of the novel occur. By some editorial miracle, totally unexplainable by either Eden, London, or ourselves, Eden's work becomes, suddenly, acceptable, and he becomes rich, famous, wanted. It would appear that Horatio Alger was right all along, success comes with hard work. Yet for Eden, material success has the taste of ashes, because it is based on "work performed." As he tells the Morses and their middle class friends at dinner, it is because he now has money and is famous that they dote on him, and not because "I'm Martin Eden, a pretty good guy and not particularly a fool... And it was all done long ago; it was work performed,... when you spat upon me as the dirt under your feet."

Considering Eden's work experiences, his denial and hatred of physical labor since his laundry experience along with his lack of mental toughness as illustrated in the Cheese Face and laundry episodes discussed above, Eden's distaste for success based on "work performed" is understandable. Within an existential philosophical system, Eden's obsession of people accepting him on the basis of "work performed" becomes clear. Eden refuses to be objectivized, to be made an "it" by others, as all of us tend to do to people. He will not be "pigeon-holed" as an artist, he wants to be taken as a man. Yet what truly crushes Eden, what really shows his lack of emotional strength, and reveals the depth of his existential problem, is Brissenden's death.

I have noted the similarities between Brissenden and Eden earlier. Neither Brissenden nor Eden have the mental strength required by an existential age of the introspective writer. They both search desperately for answers, they are both overwhelmed by the thought of man as little more than nothing in the chaos of the universe. I have shown how their physical experiences have made them apparently strong but brittle, liable to shatter emotionally at any unforeseen shock. The physical trials they have undergone have made them aware of man's weakness, his lack of strength against the universe. They have also read of man's physical and emotional limitations in the scheme of nature. Introspection has reinforced their knowledge, gained by first-hand physical experience, of man's nothingness, physically and spiritually. One is reminded of Pope's epigram concerning knowledge; both Brissenden and Eden drink deep finally, but of the Lethan, not the Pierian spring. Industrialism and science have taken away the props man had in earlier times. Brissenden and Eden, introspective and searching for an enduring philosophy of life, face the void with no solid faith to grab onto, not even an Horatio Alger myth. "Work performed" becomes a dirge because it is not enough to save Eden from destruction. Horatio Alger is too weak, and Eden is too worn out to face the battle of existence. Eden falls to an inhuman universe, as Horatio Alger falls to the existential dilemma.

There are other signs throughout the novel that Eden is heading toward a dilemma of existence, a problem of alienation. Loneliness is a continuously stated problem for Eden throughout the book. Because he is entranced and possessed by the fruit of the middle class, knowledge, Eden breaks off relations with the lower class, his first paradise. He finds the lower class too coarse, ill-mannered, and stupid, at first, to remain with them. Even after his disillusionment with the middle-class, he finds it impossible to return to the lower class, to find a woman like Lizzie Connolly satisfying and fulfilling. He recognizes her virtues and her beauty, but he is too far alienated from her surroundings to stay with her. Eden realizes he is not a brute and is "a damn poor Nietzscheman," that he would marry Lizzie if he could "and fill her quivering heart full of happiness." But Martin Eden cannot, "and it's a damn shame."

At first, the middle class is Eden's goal. But he soon becomes disillusioned with the bourgeois. They are too shallow, grasping, and frightened to interest him. Eden's relationship with Ruth is indicative of his whole relationship with middle class society. Ruth, an ironical name to give to a woman who is far from ready or willing to go wherever Eden would lead her, is at once afraid and drawn to Eden, primarily for the same reasons American "polite" society is both drawn to and afraid of him—his vitality and power are repulsive, yet magnetic to the middle class. Eden realizes this and refuses to be used. Now he finds the bourgeois "sickening," and realizes that what he dreamed in his innocence, "that the persons who sat in the high places, who lived in fine houses and had educations and bank accounts, were worthwhile," is the great lie of the Horatio Alger success story.

He moves toward the socialists, the labor unions, the radicals, but because he is already alone, because he is already divorced from two classes, he cannot accept their theories. His star is the hero, the Nietzschian superman, and socialism, while fine for the mob, is not for Martin Eden. With Brissenden's suicide, he is truly alone, alienated, the classic existential anti-hero in the classic existential dilemma. It is then that he longs for paradise again, to which he can never return, the paradise he knew as a poor sailor in Tahiti. There, he and Moti, the chief's son, wait for "the rush of a big breaker whereon to jump the reef." Eden relives those thrilling moments of breakthrough, of fierce physical enjoyment, of youthful pleasures, of agrarian order so that he can escape from the "disorder of his squalid room," from the disorder of his existential dilemma in the modern industrial world.

Eden has gone from order to disorder, from paradise to hell, from being at one with the universe to alienation from it and from his fellow man. The "Moti" dream is an aspect and outgrowth of the westering myth of escape. It is then that he attempts to return to the South Seas, to go west, to escape from his existential reality. But suicide can be spiritual as well as physical. Eden attempts death through myth, through dream, and perhaps, realizing this on a subconscious level, kills himself physically on route to his spiritual death. Because, as we have seen, he lacks the necessary mental toughness to survive in this existential world, Eden cannot face the loss of paradise to which his introspectiveness has led him. Suicide, from this desert of emotions, from this spiritual hell, becomes a positive act for Eden. He conquers the absurd natural order by imposing his human will on it, forcing himself to death. The natural order prompts him to swim, to keep alive, but Eden, rejecting life, goes to death positively, happily, willingly. Pain and strangulation was a hurt not imposed by death, since "death did not hurt. It was life, the pangs of life, this awful, suffocating feeling; it was the last blow life could deal him."

Martin Eden is a rude shock to a literature overwhelmed with the Horatio Alger-Gospel of Wealth myth. I find no other American novel of the era is so hopeless, so empty, so awful in its view of man as this one is. Long before the terminology came into existence, London had written an existential novel, had given America one of its first existential anti-heroes. Like Eden just before his death, one sees in this novel a terrible vision of self-knowledge, of self-awareness for America in the 20th century:

> It seemed a lighthouse; but it was inside his brain—a flashing, bright white light. It flashed swifter and swifter. There was a long rumble of sound, and it seemed to him that he was falling down a vast and interminable stairway. And somewhere at the bottom he fell into darkness. That much he knew. He had fallen into darkness. And at the instant he knew, he ceased to know.

Notes on Contributors

SAM S. BASKETT is Professor of English at Michigan State University. He has taught under Fulbright Grants in Mexico and Turkey and was Visiting Professor of American Literature and American Studies at Hacettepe University, Ankara, Turkey, 1977-78. He has published widely on London and other American writers. He edited the Rinehart Edition of *Martin Eden* and *The American Identity* published by D.C. Heath.

JAMES ELLIS is an associate professor of English at the University of North Carolina at Greensboro. He has published articles on late nineteenth century and twentieth century fiction in such periodicals as *American Literature, Western American Literature,* and *The Univeristy Review.*

KING HENDRICKS received his PhD from Stanford and spent most of his professional life as a teacher and English Department Head at Utah State University. He was influential in the revival of interest in London and in arranging to have London material placed in the USU library.

EARLE LABOR, professor of English at Centenary College of Louisiana, is author of *Jack London* (New York: Twayne, 1974), the first book-length critical study of London's work published in America. He is the editor of *Great Short Works of Jack London* (New York: Harper & Row, 1965: 2nd ed. rev., 1970) and served as guest editor for the special Jack London number of *Modern Fiction Studies* (Spring, 1976). He is currently at work on a definitive edition of London's correspondence in collaboration with Robert C. Leitz III and I. Milo Shepard, which will be published by the Stanford University Press.

JAMES I. MCCLINTOCK is Professor and Director of English at Lyman Briggs College, Michigan State University, East Lansing, Michigan. He has published on American writers and is the author of *White Logic: Jack London's Short Stories* (Wolf House Books: Grand Rapids, Michigan, 1975).

GORDON MILLS is Professor of English at the University of Texas at Austin. He recently published *Hamlet's Castle: The Study of Literature as a Social Experience.*

RAY OWNBEY is an Associate Professor of English and Chairman of the Humanities Division at the University of Maine at Fort Kent. He has published on Jack London and on contemporary American fiction.

JONATHAN H. SPINNER received his doctorate from Michigan State University. He has published on London, and presently resides in Danbury, Connecticut.

CLARICE STASZ is an Associate Professor of Sociology at Sonoma State College, Rohnert Park, California. She is the author of four books and numerous articles primarily in the areas of sex roles and inequality in American society. Her forthcoming biography of Charmian London is entitled *Mate-Woman: The Story of Charmian Kitteridge London.*

EARL J. WILCOX is Professor of English and Chairman of the Department of English and Drama at Winthrop College in Rock Hill, South Carolina. He has published on Jack London as well as on other American writers and is the author of *Fundamentals of Fiction* (Allyn & Bacon, 1975). He is president of the Philological Association of the Carolinas.

Bibliography

WORKS BY JACK LONDON

Novels

The Abysmal Brute. New York: Century, 1913.
Adventure. New York: Macmillan, 1911.
The Assassination Bureau, Ltd. (Completed by Robert Fish). New York: McGraw-Hill, 1963.
Before Adam. New York: Macmillan, 1907.
Burning Daylight. New York: Macmillan, 1910.
The Call of the Wild. New York: Macmillan, 1903.
The Cruise of the Dazzler. New York: Century, 1902.
A Daughter of the Snows. Philadelphia: Lippincott, 1902.
The Game. New York: Macmillan, 1905.
Hearts of Three. New York: Macmillan, 1920.
The Iron Heel. New York: Macmillan, 1908.
Jerry of the Islands. New York: Macmillan, 1917.
John Barleycorn. New York: Century, 1913.
The Little Lady of the Big House. New York: Macmillan, 1916.
Martin Eden. New York: Macmillan, 1909.
Michael, Brother of Jerry. New York: Macmillan, 1917.
The Mutiny of the Elsinore. New York: Macmillan, 1914.
The Scarlet Plague. New York: Macmillan, 1915.
The Sea Wolf. New York: Macmillan, 1904.
The Star Rover. New York: Macmillan, 1915.
The Valley of the Moon. New York: Macmillan, 1913.
White Fang. New York: Macmillan, 1906.

Stories

Children of the Frost. New York: Macmillan, 1902.
Dutch Courage and Other Stories. New York: Macmillan, 1922.
The Faith of Men. New York: Macmillan, 1904.
The God of His Fathers. New York: McClure Phillips, 1901.
The House of Pride and Other Tales of Hawaii. New York: Macmillan, 1912.
Lost Face. New York: Macmillan, 1910.
Love of Life and Other Stories. New York: Macmillan, 1907.
Moon-Face and Other Stories. New York: Macmillan, 1906.
The Night Born. New York: Century, 1913.

On the Makaloa Mat. New York: Macmillan, 1919.
The Red One. New York: Macmillan, 1918.
Smoke Bellow. New York: Century, 1912.
A Son of the Sun. Garden City, New York: Doubleday, Page, 1912.
The Son of the Wolf. Boston: Houghton Mifflin, 1900.
South Sea Tales. New York: Macmillan, 1911.
The Strength of the Strong. New York: Macmillan, 1914.
Tales of the Fish Patrol. New York: Macmillan, 1905.
The Turtles of Tasman. New York: Macmillan, 1916.
When God Laughs and Other Stories. New York: Macmillan, 1911.

Non-fiction

The Cruise of the Snark. New York: Macmillan, 1911.
The Human Drift. New York: Macmillan, 1917.
Jack London Reports. ed. King Hendricks and Irving Shephard. Garden City, New York: Doubleday, 1970.
The Kempton-Wace Letters (with Anna Strunsky). New York: Macmillan, 1903.
Letters from Jack London. ed. King Hendricks and Irving Shephard. New York: Odyssey, 1965.
The People of the Abyss. New York: Macmillan, 1903.
Revolution and Other Essays. New York: Macmillan, 1910.
War of the Classes. New York: Macmillan, 1905.

Plays

The Acorn-Planter: A California Forest Play. New York: Macmillan, 1916.
Daughters of the Rich. ed. James E. Sisson. Oakland, California: Holmes Book Company, 1971.
Gold (with Herbert Heron). ed. James E. Sisson. Oakland, California: Holmes Book Company, 1972.
Scorn of Women. New York: Macmillan, 1906.
Theft: A Play in Four Acts. New York: Macmillan, 1910.

WRITING ABOUT JACK LONDON

The works listed here provide additional material about London. The reader is referred for more complete information to the bibliographies listed below, especially those by Woodbridge and Sherman. In addition there are three journals which deal with London: the *Jack London Newsletter* which prints, among other things, addenda to Professor Woodbridge's *Jack London: A Bibliography; The London Collector* which publishes items of interest to the collector of London materials; and *What's New About London, Jack?* a co-operative effort between subscribers and the publisher which includes information of interest concerning London.

Biography

Barltrop, Robert. *Jack London: The Man, The Writer, The Rebel.* London: Pluto Press, 1976.

London, Charmian. *The Book of Jack London.* 2 volumes. New York: Century, 1921.

London, Joan. *Jack London and His Times: An Unconventional Biography.* New York: Doubleday, 1939.

O'Connor, Richard. *Jack London: A Biography.* Boston: Little, Brown, 1964.

Sinclair, Andrew. *Jack: A Biography of Jack London.* New York: Harper and Row, 1977.

Stone, Irving. *Sailor on Horseback: The Biography of Jack London.* Cambridge, Massachusetts: Houghton Mifflin, 1938. Reissued as *Irving Stone's Jack London: His Life, Sailor on Horseback (A Biography) And Twenty-Eight Selected Jack London Stories.* Garden City, New York: Doubleday, 1977.

Walker, Franklin. *Jack London and the Klondike: The Genesis of an American Writer.* San Marino, California: Huntington Library, 1966.

Bibliography

Sherman, Joan R. *Jack London: A Reference Guide.* Boston: G.K. Hall & Co., 1977.

Sisson, James E. III, comp. "Jack London's Plays: A Chronological Bibliography," in his edition of Jack London's *Daughters of the Rich.* Oakland, California: Holmes Book Company, 1971, 17-20.

__________, comp. "Jack London's Published Poems: A Chronological Bibliography." *The London Collector,* I (July, 1970), 20-21.

Walker, Dale L., comp. *The Fiction of Jack London; A Chronological Bibliography.* Research and editing by James E. Sisson, III. El Paso: Texas Western Press, 1972.

Woodbridge, Hensley C., London, John, and Tweney, George H. *Jack London: A Bibliography.* Georgetown, California: Talisman Press, 1966. Enlarged edition with "Supplement" and comprehensive index by Woodbridge, Milwood, New York: Kraus, 1970.

Criticism

Brown, Deming. "Jack London and O. Henry," *Soviet Attitudes Toward American Writing.* Princeton: Princeton University Press, 1962, 219-38.

Carroll, Lavon B. "Jack London and the American Image," *American Book Collector,* XIII (January, 1963), 23-27.

Dhondt, Steven T. " 'There is a Good Time Coming': Jack London's Spirit of Proletarian Revolt," *Jack London Newsletter,* III (January-April, 1970), 25-34.

Feied, Frederick. *No Pie in the Sky: The Hobo as American Cultural Hero in the Works of Jack London, John Dos Passos and Jack Kerouac.* New York: Citadel, 1964.

Fuller, Frank A. "*Martin Eden* and Critical Realism," *American Book Collector,* XVII (November, 1966), 19-21.

Gurian, Jay. "The Romantic Necessity in Literary Naturalism: Jack London," *American Literature,* XXXVIII (March, 1966), 112-20.

Labor, Earle. "From 'All Gold Canyon' to *The Acorn Planter:* Jack London's Agrarian Vision," *Western American Literature,* XI (August, 1977), 83-101.

__________. *Jack London.* TUSAS. New York: Twayne, 1974.

Labor, Earle and Hendricks, King. "Jack London's Twice-Told Tale," *Studies in Short Fiction,* IV (Summer, 1967), 334-41.

Mills, Gordon. "Jack London's Quest for Salvation," *American Quarterly,* VII (Spring, 1955), 3-14.

McClintock, James I. *White Logic: Jack London's Short Stories.* Grand Rapids, Michigan: Wolf House Books, 1975.

Pattee, Fred Lewis. *The Development of the American Short Story: An Historical Survey.* New York: Harper, 1923, 347-53.

Pearsall, Robert Brainard. "Elizabeth Barrett Meets Wolf Larsen," *Western American Literature,* IV (Spring, 1969), 3-13.

Shivers, Alfred S. "Jack London's Mate-Women," *American Book Collector,* XV (October, 1964), 17-21.

__________. "The Demoniacs in Jack London," *American Book Collector,* XII (September, 1961), 11-14.

Walcutt, Charles Child. "Jack London: Blond Beasts and Supermen," in *American Literary Naturalism: A Divided Stream.* Minneapolis: University of Minnesota Press, 1956.

__________. *Jack London.* Pamphlets on American Writers No. 57. Minneapolis: University of Minnesota Press, 1966.

Walker, Franklin D. "Jack London: *Martin Eden,*" in *The American Novel from James Fenimore Cooper to William Faulkner.* ed. Wallace Stegner. New York: Basic Books, 1965.

Willson, Carolyn. "'Rattling the Bones': Jack London as Social Evangelist," *Western American Literature,* XI (August, 1976), 135-48.

Yoder, Jon A. "Jack London as Wolf Barleycorn," *Western American Literature,* XI (August, 1976), 83-101.